LEARNING FROM THE OLD MASTERS

LEARNING FROM THE OLD MASTERS

by Joseph Sheppard

WATSON-GUPTILL PUBLICATIONS/NEW YORK
PITMAN PUBLISHING/LONDON

This book is written in grateful memory of my teacher
Jacques Maroger, and to Nina, Leni, and Lynn.

First published 1979 in the United States and Canada by Watson-Guptill Publications,
a division of Billboard Publications, Inc.,
1515 Broadway, New York, N.Y. 10036

Library of Congress Cataloging in Publication Data
Sheppard, Joseph, 1930–
  Learning from the old masters.
  Bibliography: p.
  Includes index.
  1. Painting—Technique. 2. Painting, Renaissance
—Techniques. 3. Painting, Modern—17th-18th
centuries—Technique. I. Title.
ND1500.S48 1979   751.4'5   79-4407
ISBN O-8230-2672-8

Published in Great Britain by Pitman Publishing Ltd.,
39 Parker Street, London WC2B 5PB
ISBN 0-273-01348-3

Manufactured in Japan

First Printing, 1979

CONTENTS

INTRODUCTION

Most artists and students are overwhelmed by the technical virtuosity of the old masters, particularly the oil painters of the late sixteenth and seventeenth centuries. Close examination of the original paintings tells us *something* about how they were painted . . . but not really enough. The paintings have been varnished, patched, restored, repainted, cleaned (or not cleaned), and mounted on new canvases. We look only at the remains of a Rubens, a Rembrandt, or a Titian. But we still think: "I'd like to be able to do that—not copy or imitate it but do my own portrait or figure and get that particular effect." If only we could slip back into the past, spend a day with Rembrandt, and ask, "Show me, tell me, how do you do it?"

This book attempts to reconstruct and demonstrate, step by step, how Dürer, Titian, Veronese, Caravaggio, Rubens, Hals, Rembrandt, and Vermeer painted portraits and figures. I have chosen these artists because I think they are the greatest painters of all time; because each of them uses somewhat different procedures and materials; and because we do have a reasonable idea of how they painted.

I hope that the artist, the teacher, and the art student will find this a more practical book than so many others that have been written on the techniques and "secret formulas" of the masters. Most of these volumes are just recipe books; their authors never really *show* you how to paint the way the masters did. And all the documents and verbal hypotheses mean nothing if in actual practice the methods do not work.

DEMONSTRATIONS

To show each artist's technique, I have painted a picture of my own. Although my subject is one that the master might have chosen, I have not tried to make a facsimile; nor have I inserted one of my heads into a master composition. Working in my own style—as, I hope, you will work in yours—I have followed the same step-by-step process that I think each master must have followed. I have tried to use similar supports, grounds, colors, and mediums—or materials that can produce effects that are *comparable* to those produced by the masters.

MEDIUMS

I will recommend a variety of painting mediums—both homemade and commercial—that will produce effects similar to those you see in the paintings of the great masters. You must experiment to discover which medium suits your style and technique. I make no claim that these mediums are, in fact, the old-master formulas. And I hasten to add that I do not think *anyone* has the exact formulas of the masters.

Actually, there seems to be no one absolute "master medium." Rubens, whose technical genius outshines all but Rembrandt's, constantly changed his medium. In the National Gallery of Art in Washington there are six Rubens paintings in one room, and among them at least three different mediums seem to have been used.

OIL

In all the demonstrations in this book I use raw linseed oil. However, the best painters worked tirelessly to render the oil as colorless as possible before they used it. The method used to clean the oil is called *washing*—tedious but worth the trouble. Whenever the word *oil* is used in a formula, I am referring to washed linseed oil. The procedure for washing the oil is given in the discussion of mediums on p. 11. I do not believe that commercial mediums contain this purified oil, so you must do the washing yourself if you want the best results.

COLORS

All the colors used in the demonstrations are the traditional blend of dry pigments and linseed oil, whether these colors are homemade or bought readymade in tubes from the art supply store. The white is always white lead—commonly called flake white—the only white used by the masters. It is very opaque; has more body than other whites; is the best white for modeling and for mixing with other colors; and forms the most durable paint film when dry. But a great deal of care must be taken in using white lead . . . it is poisonous if taken internally, whether by mouth or through a cut on your hand.

The colors I use in the demonstrations are not necessarily the exact ones used by each master. However, in selecting their colors, all these painters adhered to the same principles. They all used white lead and ivory black, which gave them the maximum contrast of light and dark; a cool yellow and a warm yellow; a cool red and a warm red; a cool blue and a warm blue; and one or more earth browns. Sometimes a green was added to the palette. The wooden palette was small, containing only a few colors, and these colors were usually mixed directly on the canvas.

Starting from left to right my palette is laid out with white, yellows, reds, browns, black, and blues. I place my own medium, which has the consistency of jelly, in the center of the palette and use it to dilute my colors, which I place around the edge of the palette. Instructions for making my medium—and other painting mediums—are given in the text that follows this Introduction. In the demonstrations I list my colors in the order in which I lay them out on my palette.

GROUNDS

I give several formulas for grounds, some old and some new. A good painting surface is one that is nonabsorbent, has sufficient "tooth" (or texture) to take the brush stroke, and allows the paint to hold fast and dry well. Besides the instructions I give for making grounds in the section on painting surfaces, beginning page 22, there are further suggestions about painting surfaces in the brief introductions to the demonstrations.

8

BRUSHES

The larger the brush, the easier it is to cover a surface. I prefer bristles over soft-hair brushes. Bristles hold more paint, make a more visible stroke, and can make anything from a fine line to a layer of heavy color. It is important to have a lot of good brushes of different sizes—and keep them clean. After painting, wipe the paint off the brushes with a cloth or a paper towel, then wash them in mild soap and warm water. Do not simply rinse brushes in turpentine, which ruins the bristles.

As you paint, each color should be assigned its own brush, even several brushes of different sizes. Only by doing this can you paint one color over another without creating mud.

In the introduction to each demonstration I list the brushes I use for that demonstration.

USING THIS BOOK

To get the most out of this book, I suggest that you try the recommended colors, mediums, and brushes, paying special attention to the method of canvas or panel preparation.

Study each demonstration step by step and try a similar procedure in a painting of your own. Substitute your own model or, if you prefer, copy the painting in the book. After all, this book is not about the *creative* part of painting but simply about the *technical* part. The important thing is not your finished picture but the knowledge and experience you gain from working in these techniques.

If your local museum permits copying, contact the museum administration for permission to set up your easel and work in the galleries. The ideal way to learn the technique of a specific master is to copy one of his originals.

FURTHER READING

There are certainly other books worth reading.

Jacques Maroger, a noted restorer and my teacher for fifteen years, wrote *The Secret Formulas and Techniques of the Masters* (see the Bibliography), in which he claimed to give the formulas of the painting mediums used by great artists, from the Van Eycks to Velasquez. But years after writing the book, he was still revising the recipes. I think he was correct on the techniques of Rubens and many of the other artists, but his formulas for mediums never seemed quite right. However, the main point about the controversial Maroger medium is that it works. It may not really be the Rubens medium, but one can paint with it—and very well indeed.

Since artists began to paint, there have been books written on techniques and materials, though it is often difficult to get clear information from these books. Many of the old ones are now in paperback editions. Some of the best-known authors are Vasari, Van Mander, Cennini, Eastlake, and Cooke. I give a list of their books at the end of this volume.

MATERIALS
AND FORMULAS

MEDIUMS

It is almost impossible to paint fine pictures in oil without using some kind of medium. I find the commonly used mixtures of raw linseed oil and turpentine inadequate as mediums because they tend to make colors become muddy; they are too thin and tend to run; and they dry to a dull finish. There are commercial mediums available, which I describe later in this section, but I am not completely satisfied with the results they give either. The mediums that work best for me are those I make myself from various formulas, which I describe in the pages that follow. Admittedly, it takes more time to concoct a medium than to buy a commercial formula, but I find homemade products more satisfying because of the results I can attain with them. As you work with this book, I recommend that you try the mediums I use, as well as a number of the others listed. Only by experimenting can you find the specific ones that work best for you.

I use one basic medium—and a variation of it—for the demonstrations in this book. Over the years that I have been experimenting with various mediums and with the techniques used by the old masters, these are the mediums I have found to work best for me. I make no claims that these are the exact formulas used by the master painters represented here, since, as I have said earlier, I do not think *anyone* knows the exact formulas. But the properties of these mediums—such as consistency, drying time, and the way in which they combine with colors—make it possible to follow the procedures that the old masters seem to have used.

In this section I begin with a discussion of linseed oil, the technique of washing oil, and the method of making black oil (since such knowledge is essential to making the basic medium); then I tell you how to make this basic medium and a variation of it.

LINSEED OIL

A major element in every medium is some kind of oil. The oils most commonly used by the masters were walnut oil, poppy oil, and linseed oil. Cold-pressed raw linseed oil was usually preferred over the others, and that is what I recommend that you use in making your own mediums. Cold-pressed raw linseed oil is admittedly quite expensive, but it *is* the best. Commercial linseed oil—the kind used by house painters—is not suitable, since it has been purified by a chemical process. Therefore, I suggest that you buy raw linseed oil and *wash* it—a process for purifying oil that I describe below. It is possible to use the linseed oil without washing it, but your results will be much more satisfying if you do.

One drawback to oil painting is that after a time the oil in the finished painting may darken if the picture is stored in a place without light or merely hung in a dark place. This can be remedied, however, by placing the painting in the sun for bleaching. After a few days the oil will bleach back to its original brightness.

WASHING LINSEED OIL

The great artists of the past did everything they could to make their oil as colorless and free of mucilage as possible. (Mucilage is a gelatinous, grayish, cloudy substance in the oil, which the masters considered a major cause of darkening.) The most common method of purifying the oil was known as washing, and it was believed that this process made oil paintings more permanent. Here are the steps to follow for two washing methods.

First Method

1.   Fill a large, clear glass jar with a lid one-third with water and one-third with oil.

2.   Shake the jar thoroughly until the water and oil combine. A little salt or sand added to the mixture before you shake it will accelerate the washing process because the salt or sand pulls out the mucilage and causes it to settle at the bottom of the jar. However, water alone is sufficient.

3.   Let the mixture sit. After a few hours three layers of liquid will be visible: The top layer is oil; the middle layer is mucilage; and the bottom layer is water.

4.   Shake the mixture twice a day for seven days.

5.   To separate out the oil, pour the mixture into a pan, let the fluids settle into three layers, and then freeze the contents of the pan. Once the water freezes, the mucilage freezes with it and the oil can then be poured off the top.

6.   These steps can be repeated until the oil is clear and there is no more mucilage.

Second Method

1.   Find a container that has a spout on the side and toward the bottom—such as a coffee urn or a samovar or a large picnic thermos. Make sure that the spout can be opened easily and shut tightly.

2.   Fill two thirds of the container with a 50–50 mixture of oil and water.

3.   Shake the container until the two liquids are thoroughly mixed.

4.   Let the mixture sit until the oil separates and floats to the top.

5.   Open the spout and very gradually let the water drain out. First the mucilage will run out along with the water. As soon as the *oil* begins to come out, close the stopper quickly.

6.   Repeat the process as many times as are needed for the oil to become clear.

Whichever washing process you use, do *not* pour the mucilage down the sink or into the toilet. Put the mucilage in a jar or a can and dispose of it with your trash.

SUN-THICKENED OIL AND STAND OIL

In some of the alternative mediums that I list later in this section, sun-thickened oil and stand oil turn up as ingredients. Linseed oil is processed by heat to produce these thick, honeylike oils, which lend a heavy fluid consistency to your paint—and dry to a tougher film than raw oil.

TURPENTINE

A standard ingredient in most painting mediums, turpentine is a mild solvent that makes mediums thinner. It is sold in art supply stores under such names as essential oil of turpentine, essence of turpentine, or spirits of turpentine.

VENICE TURPENTINE

Venice turpentine is a viscous balsam that comes from trees; it is *not* a substitute for ordinary turpentine. Venice turpentine spreads slightly after it has been placed on a painting surface. In my demonstration of the techniques of Vermeer I pick up a few drops of Venice turpentine on my palette knife and stir this interesting additive into the medium. The diffused highlights of the portrait are achieved not by blending but by simply adding Venice turpentine.

MAKING BLACK OIL

Black oil is the basis of the mediums I use in all the demonstrations in this book. The small amount of lead in black oil makes all my colors—when diluted with medium—behave as white lead oil paint behaves. The black oil makes the colors creamy, gives them good brushing qualities, speeds drying, and gives the colors both fluidity and holding strength—the colors stay where you put them. Black oil can also be used for grinding your own colors with dry pigments—which I will say more about in a moment—and as a diluent.

One of the necessary ingredients for making black oil is litharge, a form of pure lead that can be purchased in most hardware stores. It is an orange powder that behaves in the same way as powdered white lead pigment and can be used in the same proportions. If you use either litharge or powdered white lead pigment, be careful not to breathe in the powdered particles as you work. They are *poisonous.*

An alternative to using these powdered forms of lead is white lead paste, often called "white lead in oil," which comes in a can; it can also be purchased in a hardware or paint store. The percentage of lead in the paste varies with the brands available, so you will have to experiment with the proportions in the recipes that follow. As you try different proportions and test them in your paintings, you can decide what consistency you want your black oil to be.

linseed oil—20 parts
litharge *or* powdered white lead pigment or white lead paste—1 part

1. Measure proportions by weight, not by volume.

2. Mix the oil and litharge or white lead powdered pigment or paste in a large porcelain pot.

3. Place a thin asbestos pad over a low flame, then place the porcelain pot on the pad. The asbestos pad—which insures that the pot heats evenly—can be purchased in most stores that sell kitchen supplies.

4. Cook the mixture, stirring occasionally with a wooden spoon, until the temperature reaches 250° F (120° C). Check the temperature with a cooking thermometer.

5. After the oil turns a clear, coffee-colored black, let it cook for one hour. Do not let it boil. If the oil becomes too hot, remove it from the fire and let it cool a bit before placing it back on the heat.

6. When the cooking time is completed, let the oil sit until it cools to room temperature. Then pour it into bottles and seal them.

7. In a few days some undissolved lead will settle at the bottom of the bottles. Do not shake the bottle after this.

SAFETY PRECAUTIONS

As already noted, do not breathe in the powdered white lead or litharge particles while working with them. Also, do not eat or smoke while working with the ingredients or while painting with the oil. Avoid getting the mixture or the ingredients into any cut on the skin.

All mediums should be cooked with open ventilation and in either an earthenware or porcelain pot. A lid for the pot should be kept near your work area; if the oil should ignite, the fire can easily be smothered by placing the lid on the pot. It is also extremely important to keep any form of water away from the hot oil. A small dry chemical fire extinguisher (or just a package of baking soda) produces instant results if the oil should spill *and* ignite.

BASIC DEMONSTRATION MEDIUM

I use this medium in the demonstrations of the techniques of Dürer, Titian, Veronese, Caravaggio, and Hals. Most of my students like this medium because it models well, stays workable for a long sitting of four or five hours, and dries to the touch overnight.

In its final form this medium becomes a jelly, which you can mix with your tube colors, using a palette knife or brush, to thin the paint and improve the brushing consistency of the colors. The medium *looks* as thick as the paint but is actually much softer. When paint is diluted with this medium, its color becomes soft and buttery. This jelly medium can be diluted with raw linseed oil (preferably washed) to make the medium more liquid and to slow down the drying time. I do not recommend mixing turpentine with this medium; turpentine breaks down the adhesiveness of the paint.

Make only enough medium for one or two months' painting, since its good qualities are lost with the passage of time.

This medium calls for an ingredient called *mastic,* a natural resin that makes paint more luminous. Mastic comes in small crystals resembling rock candy; these crystals are called mastic tears and are sold, already cleaned, in Greek grocery stores under the name "mastica." If you buy mastic tears in an art supply store, they may be dirty or dusty; to clean off the dust, place them in a small bag or a sock and then shake it.

> linseed oil—20 parts
> litharge *or* powdered white lead pigment or white lead paste—1 part
> turpentine—20 parts
> mastic tears—7 parts

1. Measure proportions by weight, not by volume.

2. Using the linseed oil and litharge or white lead powdered pigment or paste, follow steps 1–4 of the directions for making black oil found on page 12. This will prepare the oil for the remaining steps in the recipe for this particular medium.

3. Pour the turpentine into as many small wide-mouthed jars as you need—jelly jars or instant coffee jars will do nicely. Fill each jar a little less than half full. Put them aside for later use.

4. Allow the prepared oil to cook 200° F (94° C). Place the pot containing the oil over a flame low enough to maintain this temperature. Check the temperature with a cooking thermometer as you work.

5. Slowly sprinkle in the clear mastic tears, stirring constantly to keep the mastic from sticking to the bottom of the pot. As soon as the mastic has dissolved, turn off the fire.

6. Pour the mixture into the jars that you half filled with turpentine. This mixture should jell almost immediately. If it does not, leave it overnight; by morning the medium will be a jelly. Seal the jars tightly.

Before you start to paint, you can add a very small amount of this medium to each tube color on your palette except white lead (flake white). Use just enough medium to cover the tip of your knife or brush—you will find that a little medium goes a long way. Or you can place the medium in the center of your palette and dilute your colors as you work. Or you can do *both.*

VARIATION OF THE BASIC MEDIUM

I use this medium in the demonstrations of the techniques of Rubens, Rembrandt, and Vermeer. It varies from the basic medium only in the proportions of the ingredients used. I personally prefer this variation to the basic medium itself because it suits my particular painting style very well. The variation is much thicker than the basic medium, becomes tacky more quickly, and dries sooner. This suits me because I paint rapidly.

This medium sets up well and dries in a few hours. Maximum working time in one area is two to three hours. The paint dries to the touch in twelve hours. If you find this medium too difficult to handle because of its rapid drying, you can extend the working period by using half the amount of litharge. You can also add raw linseed oil to thin it and to slow its drying time as you are working. As with the basic medium, you can mix this medium with each color on your palette (except white lead) and place some in the center of your palette to use as a diluent while painting.

> linseed oil—10 parts
> litharge *or* powdered white lead pigment or white lead paste—1 part
> turpentine—10 parts
> mastic tears—10 parts

1. Measure proportions by weight, not by volume.

2. Follow the directions on page 14 for making the basic medium, using the proportions given above.

VAN DYCK MEDIUM

As a matter of historical interest, here is a formula from the time of Van Dyck, recorded by an unknown writer and published in Eastlake's *Methods and Materials of Painting of the Great Schools and Masters* (see the Bibliography). This medium is a combination of drying oil and varnish. The instructions for making this medium are somewhat sketchily recorded, and I do *not* really recommend that you try it. The steps that follow seem to be the order in which the medium was originally made.

Drying Oil

> white lead—1½–2 ounces
> nut oil—1 pint

1. Measure proportions by volume, not by weight.

2. Place the nut oil in an earthenware pot. Warm over moderate heat.

3. Add the lead slowly until it is dissolved in the oil.

4. Take the pot off the fire, and let the oil-lead mixture cool.

5. Clarify the oil by straining it and letting it stand.

6. Use the oil fresh. It should not be kept longer than a month.

Mastic Varnish

> gum mastic—1 pound
> turpentine—2 pounds
> drying oil—½ pint

1. Measure proportions by volume, not by weight.

2. Place the gum mastic and the turpentine in an earthenware pot. Heat the two until the mastic is dissolved, but do not allow the mixture to boil.

3. Remove pot from heat source and allow the mixture to cool.

4. Strain out any impurities in the mixture.

5. Pour the mixture and the oil into a jar, and shake it to mix them thoroughly.

6. Pour this mixture into a pot and warm on the fire for a quarter of an hour.

7. Allow the mixture to cool. It will turn into a white jelly.

MAROGER'S "ITALIAN MEDIUM"

Maroger's *The Secret Formulas and Techniques of the Masters* describes the "Italian medium," a lead and wax formula for use with tube colors. The medium dries overnight and produces a matte finish, which tends to be somewhat opaque because of the wax. It can be used in the same way as the basic medium, that is, as a medium to mix with colors and as a diluent to be placed in the center of your palette. This medium can be mixed with white lead.

> linseed oil—10 parts
> litharge *or* powdered white lead pigment or white lead paste—1 part
> beeswax—1 part

1. Measure proportions by weight, not by volume

2. First mix the litharge or white lead powdered pigment or paste with a little oil, then add the rest of the oil.

3. Heat the mixture over a fire until it reaches 250° F (120° C). When the mixture turns black, remove from the heat.

4. Allow the mixture to cool to 145° F (65° C) and then add the beeswax. Cook the mixture, maintaining this low temperature, until the wax is melted and completely blended with the oil.

MASTIC VARNISH

This varnish is an ingredient in the medium that follows, Maroger's so-called "Rubens medium."

> mastic tears—1 part
> turpentine—2 parts

1. Measure proportions by weight, not by volume.

2. Mix the mastic tears and the turpentine in a jar, then seal it.

3. Expose the mixture to the sun for several days, turning the jar occa-

sionally. The sun will eventually dissolve the mastic, leaving a deposit in the bottom of the jar. If there is no sun at the time you make this varnish, dissolve the mastic in a double boiler, being careful to not let the mixture boil.

4.   Decant the varnish into a clear bottle, being careful to leave behind the mastic deposit that has formed. Seal the bottle tightly.

5.   To thin this varnish, you can add turpentine. The amount of turpentine will depend on how thin you want the varnish to be—and how thin you want the medium to be.

MAROGER'S "RUBENS MEDIUM"

This medium is also found in Maroger's book. The formula produces a shiny, luminous surface that is more transparent than that produced with a wax medium; however, it does not dry quite as fast, thus staying wet enough to work with all day. The surface will probably not be dry the next day and will remain too tacky to work on until the *third* day.

black oil—1 part
mastic varnish—1 part

1.   Measure proportions by weight, not by volume.

2.   Make black oil as described on page 12.

3.   Mix the oil either with commercially made mastic varnish—which can be purchased in an art supply store—or with the homemade mastic varnish just described.

BEESWAX MEDIUM

I add pure beeswax to the mediums I use in the demonstrations for the techniques of Titian and Veronese. The yellow variety of wax is preferable to the white. This wax medium gives durability and flexibility to the paint, as well as imparting to it a soft, buttery quality. The wax gives colors more body and produces a matte look.

yellow beeswax—1 part
linseed oil or black oil—3 parts

1.   Measure proportions by weight, not by volume.

2.   If you use black oil, make it as described on page 12.

3.   Place the beeswax and the black oil or linseed oil in a porcelain pot. Place pot over a low fire, heating to 145° F (65° C). When the wax is melted, and the oil and wax are completely blended, the medium is ready.

4.   Allow the mixture to cool, then place it in a jar.

SIMPLE HOMEMADE MEDIUMS

For those of you who prefer not to become involved in "cooking," there are some simple mediums that you can make yourself from readymade ingredients that you can buy in any reasonably well stocked art supply store. These formulas require nothing more than pouring the ingredients into a jar and stirring or shaking until the components are smoothly blended. Obviously, the "cooked" mediums are my first choice, but not everyone has the time or the patience to concoct these formulas. Nor does everyone share my enthusiasm for black oil, which some authorities still consider controversial. So here are some alternative mediums that are worth trying. By experimentation, you will discover which ones work best for you.

In his renowned book *The Artist's Handbook,* generally regarded as the basic reference volume on painting materials, Ralph Mayer recommends the following formula "as the best for general, all-around purposes." He points out that the amount of varnish and oil can be adjusted slightly to suit the artist's own purposes. Also a bit more turpentine can be added to make the medium more fluid.

> stand oil—1 fluid ounce
> damar varnish—1 fluid ounce
> pure gum turpentine—5 fluid ounces
> cobalt drier—about 15 drops

Mayer also recommends this medium, which contains a higher proportion of damar, plus Venice turpentine. Presumably, the measurements are by volume. Notice that the cobalt drier is omitted—the higher percentage of damar varnish will speed drying.

> damar varnish—9 parts
> turpentine—9 parts
> stand oil—4 parts
> Venice turpentine—2 parts

Mayer points out that sun-thickened oil dries faster than stand oil. He recommends the following formula as a "glaze medium," which I assume means that the medium would be particularly suitable for fluid, transparent, or semitransparent painting.

> damar varnish—4 parts
> sun-thickened linseed oil—2 parts
> Venice turpentine—1 part
> turpentine—4 parts

In Europe mastic varnish is often easier to find than damar varnish, so you may wish to substitute mastic for damar in these formulas. Both are so-called "soft resins," which means that they dissolve easily in turpentine and behave in similar ways in painting mediums.

COMMERCIAL MEDIUMS

Finally, for the reader who prefers to buy his painting mediums readymade, there *are* manufactured mediums sold in art supply stores. Although I strongly recommend that you make your own mediums to suit your own painting style, I must admit that many artists and students are perfectly happy with these commercial products. Here are some of the better ones.

Roberson's Medium for Oil Painting. According to Mayer, this is a nineteenth-century British formula containing oil, resin, and wax. It's a British product that is easy to find in the United Kingdom, but it may not be so easy to find in the United States.

Medium Flamand and Medium Venetian. These two mediums are manufactured by the French firm Le Franc and Bourgeois.

Taubes Copal Painting Medium. The noted painter and author Frederic Taubes believes that the old masters worked with so-called hard resins like copal, which resist solvents when the paint film dries, rather than with the more soluble "soft resins" like damar and mastic. His copal mediums come in three consistencies—heavy, medium, and light—and are manufactured by the American firm Permanent Pigments and widely sold throughout the United States.

Winsor & Newton Alkyd Mediums. Even though Winsor & Newton is a British firm, its products are widely sold on both sides of the Atlantic. Alkyd is described by the manufacturer as an oil-modified synthetic resin and is sold in three consistencies: a fluid form called Liquin; a gel called Win-Gel; and a thicker gel called Oleopasto. The latter two are sold in tubes. All three accelerate drying.

Roberson's medium can be obtained from C. Roberson & Company Ltd., 71 Parkway London NW1 7QJ, England.

COLORS

Most painters of the sixteenth and seventeenth centuries used small palettes and just a few colors. This can be deduced from the palettes shown in many existing self-portraits of the artists at their easels. They did not need large palettes, since they did most of their mixing directly on the canvas or panel on which they were working. They simply placed a small amount of one color on the canvas; then added a small amount of another color to the painting surface; and finally mixed them together with the brush as they painted. I recommend that you try this if you are not in the habit of painting this way—your colors will look livelier and more irregular. But remember, the masters *rarely* used large amounts of paint on the canvas at one time. They worked with very thin paint and built it up gradually.

The colors I use in the various demonstrations are my own choices and are not necessarily the same ones used by the masters. Color choice is a very personal thing, and you must find the palette of colors that best suits your temperament and painting style.

POWDERED PIGMENTS

I prefer to make my own colors with powdered pigment and oil because I find the colors purer and brighter than commercial tube colors. Furthermore, the consistency of the paint is left up to me. Also, homemade colors do not contain the chemical additives found in commercial tube colors.

The process of "grinding" colors is surprisingly simple. A palette knife or a tool called a muller blends dry pigment and linseed oil on a slab of marble or glass. You will find detailed instructions in Ralph Mayer's *The Artist's Handbook* and Frederic Taubes's *The Painters Dictionary*.

I recommend grinding colors each day, making just enough for each sitting. A little medium can be added to each color to make the paint more consistent. Colors can also be ground in black oil, but if you do this, make sure that you use enough oil to keep the colors from drying out too quickly.

I list here the colors I make from powdered pigments. These can all be obtained in powder form from Fezandie and Sperrle in the United States and from Winsor & Newton in Britain.

alizarin crimson
burnt sienna
burnt umber
chrome yellow light
French vermilion light
ivory black
Naples yellow
Prussian blue
raw umber
ultramarine blue
white lead (flake white)
yellow ochre light

COMMERCIAL TUBE COLORS

Many readers will want to use commercial tube colors rather than making their own colors from powdered pigments and oil. If you are going to use commercial tube colors, I recommend only those that have been ground in linseed oil. I consider the following tube colors most useful:

alizarin crimson
burnt sienna
burnt umber
cadmium red
cadmium yellow
cerulean blue
chrome yellow
ivory black
Naples yellow
Prussian blue
raw sienna
raw umber
rose madder
red ochre
ultramarine blue
vermilion
white lead (flake white)
yellow ochre

You will notice that I include no greens. An excellent variety of greens can be mixed with combinations of yellows and blues, or yellows and black. Two important colors are irreplaceable: white lead (flake white) and ivory black. White lead is an absolute necessity: no other white has comparable body or opacity. Ivory black is recommended because it is transparent, an essential quality for the techniques of the masters.

Materials can be obtained from Fezandie and Sperrle at 111 Eighth Avenue, New York, N.Y. 10011. Telephone: (212) 924-1905. A free list of available materials, with current prices included, is available.

Winsor & Newton and Grumbacher also manufacture powdered pigments, which you can obtain through local art supply stores. Materials can be obtained from Winsor & Newton in Britain at London HA3 5RH, England.

SURFACES

The old masters usually painted either on canvas or on wood panels, which are called the *support*. Over this support goes a *size*, which makes the support nonabsorbent so the oil does not soak in and rot the canvas or wood. Finally, the canvas or panel is *primed, which means that the size is covered with a ground*—a white layer of white lead oil paint or gesso (more about this in a moment) on which the artist paints. The white lead or gesso is usually applied in several coats; the final coat is often toned with an earth color, a soft gray, or some other color that will enhance the finished painting.

RABBIT SKIN GLUE

Rabbit skin glue is a size that is used to fill in the fibers and seal the surface of the panel or the canvas. The proportions of the ingredients are measured by weight and can vary from 1 part glue to 15–50 parts water, depending upon how thick you wish the glue to be.

dry glue—1 part
water—15 parts

1. Place the dry glue and the water in a large porcelain or earthenware pot. Let the glue soak until it swells up and floats to the top.

2. Place the mixture over a low fire (preferably in a double boiler). Stir with a wooden spoon until the glue dissolves. Allow the mixture to remain on the fire only a short time. Do *not* let it boil.

3. Remove the mixture from the fire and let it cool. When the glue cools, it becomes a jelly. It should be stored in a jar and kept in a refrigerator to preserve it.

4. To liquify the jelly, warm it again over a low flame—never let it boil.

TRADITIONAL GESSO

The old masters used a blend of glue size and chalk—called whiting—to coat their wood panels after the preliminary coat of glue had dried. This ground works well on a rigid panel of wood or modern hardboard but is too brittle for canvas, which is so flexible that the gesso is inclined to crack or flake off. To make traditional gesso, simply warm the liquid or jellied glue on a low flame—preferably in a double boiler—and stir in an equal quantity of whiting.

ACRYLIC GESSO

A modern equivalent of the traditional gesso is acrylic gesso, a blend of white pigment and acrylic, a plastic resin that serves the same function as the liquid glue in the old formula. The acrylic binds the white pigment firmly to the painting surface.

You can buy acrylic gesso in jars or cans in any art supply store. The thick, white, pasty compound can be diluted with water to any consistency you prefer. Acrylic gesso is flexible enough for use on canvas, as well as on a panel. I generally use Liquitex gesso.

PANELS

Wood is the best support for a panel, but properly seasoned wood is difficult to come by. Untempered Masonite and marine plywood are good substitutes.

TRADITIONAL GESSO GROUND ON A PANEL

1.   Using a large brush, apply a coat of warm, liquid glue size on *each* side of the panel and allow the glue to dry. Coating both sides prevents warping.

2.   Give your panel three or four coats of gesso on each side, sanding after each coat. Keep the gesso lukewarm in a double boiler as you work. Dampen each dry coat of gesso before you add the next coat.

3.   To isolate the gesso from your paint, brush on a final coat of warm rabbit skin glue that is 1 part glue to 30 parts water. You can tint the glue with a water-based color such as a watercolor, acrylic, casein, or even poster color; paint on the tinted glue with a wide brush. Leave the striations of the brush visible if you like (as in the demonstration of the Rubens technique), since they break up the reflected light and show through the transparent shadow areas.

4.   The panel can be painted on as soon as the glue dries.

GESSO-AND-OIL GROUND ON A PANEL

1.   Using a large brush, apply a coat of warm liquid glue size on each side of the panel.

2.   Give each side of the panel three or four coats of warm gesso, sanding after each coat. Allow the gesso to dry thoroughly. After each coat dries, remember to wet it before applying the next coat.

3.   Dilute white lead oil paint with turpentine to give a creamy consistency. Then paint on a coat of the prepared paint and leave it to dry.

4.   To tone your panel, paint on a final coat of transparent color, using a mixture of your medium, the oil color of your choice, and a drop of Japan drier.

5.   When the panel is dry, it is ready for use.

CANVAS

Painting on canvas generally requires more paint than does painting on a panel because of the roughness and absorbency of the fabric. Paint does not sink into a board but sits on the surface; that is why the masters preferred panels for quick, transparent painting. However, canvas is better for painters who work slowly and build up a lot of paint.

The best ground on canvas is a flexible coat of white lead or acrylic gesso—not the brittle, traditional gesso.

PREPARING RAW CANVAS WITH WHITE LEAD

1.   Paint one coat of warm liquid rabbit skin glue (1 part dry glue to 15 parts water) on a stretched raw linen canvas. Allow the glue to dry.

2.   With the palm of your hand, rub jellied rabbit skin glue (1 part dry glue to 15 parts water) into the surface of the canvas and down into the interstices of the weave.

3.   Scrape off the excess glue with a palette knife.

4.   When the glue is dry, sand off the irregularities that stick up from the canvas.

5.   Make a paste of commercially prepared white lead in oil—as it is called in the hardware or paint store—diluted with a little turpentine, and apply it to the canvas with the flat underside of a palette knife. Press the white lead into the canvas, filling in all the gaps. Scrape off the excess with the edge of the palette knife.

6.   Repeat step 5 two or three times.

7.   Apply a final coat of 4 parts white lead in oil and 1 part medium in the same manner as in step 5, scraping the canvas as smooth as possible.

8.   Allow this final coat to dry for a few days before painting on it.

PREPARING CANVAS OR PANEL WITH ACRYLIC GESSO

1.   If you are working with canvas, first size it as described in steps 1–5 immediately above, using one coat of warm liquid glue and then one coat of jellied glue. When the size is dry, sand it. Then go on to step 2 below. Note: if you wish, you can skip this preliminary sizing and go straight to the gesso; but remember, canvas soaks up gesso, which becomes very expensive. Using a glue size first is more economical. A panel needs no size before you apply the acrylic gesso.

2.   Give the surface of the canvas or panel four or five coats of acrylic gesso, sanding each layer after it has dried. Each coat should be painted on with a large brush and at a right angle to the previous coat.

3.   Paint on a final coat of 1 part acrylic matte medium and 2 parts acrylic gesso, tinted with a tone of your choice—acrylic or watercolor. When the surface is *bone dry,* it is ready for painting.

COMMERCIALLY PREPARED BOARD AND CANVAS

Commercially prepared boards and canvases come with a readymade white ground. I have generally found them unsuitable, since they are too absorbent. If you use this type of painting surface, you must first paint on an additional layer to make the surface nonabsorbent. You can use a coat of white lead toned with the oil color of your choice. The best tones are middle values made from white lead tinted with black or with one of the umbers or ochres.

DEMONSTRATIONS OF TECHNIQUES

LIGHT AND SHADE

The old masters discovered that one light source, preferably high and slightly to the front and side, gives the best illumination for creating depth and form. Most of these painters used a light that would give them three-quarters light and one-quarter shadow on their subjects. However, certain artists such as Rubens and Titian moved the light around to the front of the model to produce a larger area of light. This gave them more color but made rendering three-dimensional form more difficult, and only the better draftsmen attempted to paint almost full light on the subject.

If a head or body is lit from above and to one side, several areas of light and shade are created. Throughout the demonstrations that follow, I'll be using certain words to describe the effects of light and shade on form. Basically, heads and figures—and three-dimensional forms in general—are divided into two major areas, the light area and the shadow area.

The light area in turn is divided into two areas: a predominant area called the *middle tone,* where the color of the object is most apparent, and the *highlight,* which is the brightest section in the area of the middle tone. The highlight is closer to the light and distinctly lighter than the middle tone.

The area turned away from the light is the shadow area and is also divided into two tones—a darker tone called the *shadow accent,* which is next to the middle tone, and a paler tone called the *reflected light,* which is light that bounces off other objects or off the background and back to the subject. It is important to remember that reflected light is never as bright as the areas in the light.

Finally, there is a tone called the *cast shadow,* which is the shadow cast by one form on another. It is darkest where it abuts the object that casts the shadow. As the cast shadow recedes from the object, the tone grows paler, softer, and more diffused. The darkest tone in the cast shadow is comparable to the shadow accent, while the paler tone in the cast shadow would be comparable to the reflected light.

To summarize, proceeding in order of value from the very lightest tones to the very darkest ones, there is the highlight, the middletone, the reflected light, the cast shadow, and the shadow accent. The drawings on pages 29 and 30 illustrate what these terms mean. The drawings on page 31 illustrate the sequence in which I usually paint in these areas of light and shade when I paint a portrait or figure.

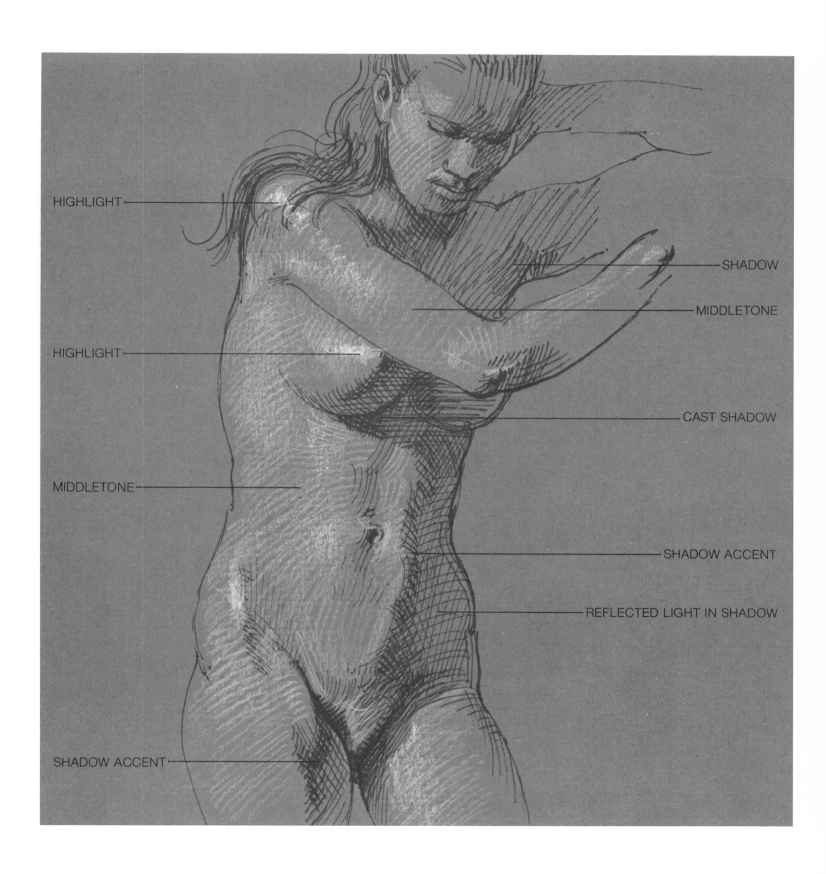

HIGHLIGHT

SHADOW

MIDDLETONE

HIGHLIGHT

CAST SHADOW

MIDDLETONE

SHADOW ACCENT

REFLECTED LIGHT IN SHADOW

SHADOW ACCENT

HIGHLIGHT

SHADOW

MIDDLETONE

SHADOW ACCENT

CAST SHADOW

SHADOW

REFLECTED LIGHT

HIGHLIGHT

REFLECTED LIGHT IN SHADOW

CAST SHADOW

MIDDLETONE

The five drawings shown here illustrate the sequence I follow in most of the demonstrations. I first draw in the *outline* of the form, establishing accurate placement of the features. I then paint in the *flat shadow areas* where the form turns away from the light. I paint in the *middletone* areas and then add the strong *shadow accents*. Finally, I place in the *highlights*—the brightest area in the middletone.

Outline

Flat shadow areas

Middletone areas

Shadow accents

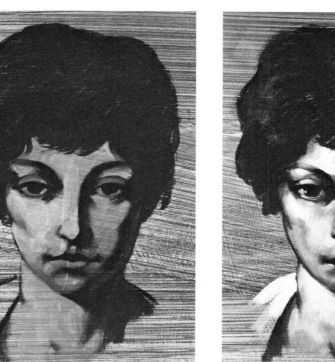

Highlights

TECHNIQUES OF
DÜRER

Albrecht Dürer (1471–1528), the greatest German artist, was one of the first painters to combine the old sharp-focus egg tempera technique and the new oil mediums developed by the Van Eycks in the early fifteenth century. With these new mediums, color became brilliant and transparent, and the artist was able to achieve subtle effects of light and to render objects in detail.

Dürer is also credited with introducing the ideas of the Italian Renaissance into Northern Europe. He made several trips to Italy, where he met Giovanni Bellini—from whom he probably learned his oil technique—and Mantegna, who also inspired him.

Dürer's enormous output included paintings, drawings, and the woodcuts and engravings that carried his fame all over Europe. He also wrote treatises on measurements, fortifications, proportion, and theory.

He prepared his paintings very deliberately and executed them carefully, modeling and filling in forms that were originally conceived in sharp outlines. He used some aerial perspective—the gradual fading of tones and colors as they recede into the distance, but his use of hard edges limited the illusion of depth. The *sfumato,* or smokelike edge, was developed later in the more free techniques of Giorgione and Titian.

For the purposes of this book, Dürer exemplifies the Flemish technique that was introduced by the Van Eyck brothers and spread throughout Northern Europe.

MEDIUM

Dürer's medium seems to have been very thin and fluid; he did not build up paint anywhere. His paintings are on wood panels. The light-colored ground shows through the transparent paint. An inner light (from the traditional gesso priming) seems to show through his colors. Shadows and lights are transparent. Only the ultimate highlight is slightly more opaque. For this demonstration I use the basic medium described on page 13.

PAINTING SURFACE

Dürer painted on wood panels that were heavily primed with many coats of traditional glue gesso. Obviously, he never used the modern gesso that I use to prepare my panel in this demonstration, but it is a good substitute for his painting surface. In this demonstration I paint on ¼″ untempered Masonite. Here are the steps to follow in preparing a panel like mine.

1.   Give the smooth side of the masonite one coat of acrylic gesso with a large flat brush. When dry, sand slightly. Paint the back too.

2.   Repeat step 1 two or three times, each time painting in a different direction and sanding after each coat. Succeeding coats should be at right angles to one another.

3.   Trace your original drawing onto transparent tracing paper and rub burnt umber pigment or pastel on the back.

4. Tape the tracing paper onto the gesso panel with the drawing side up. Go over your outline with a sharp instrument. Before you remove the tracing paper, lift a corner to see if the image has been transferred.

5. Once the image is on the gesso, draw over it and strengthen the modeling with pen and ink.

6. Paint over the panel with a mixture of medium tinted with yellow ochre and burnt umber, and a drop of Japan drier. The coat of medium fixes the drawing and makes the board nonabsorbent.

7. Before painting, let the panel sit for a few days until thoroughly dry.

PROBABLE WORKING SEQUENCE

Dürer made a careful chalk drawing from life and then probably made a copy in the exact size of the painting. He then transferred the image to his gesso panel just as I described in steps 3 to 5 above. He fixed the drawing with transparent varnish or medium, usually tinted with a flesh color. When the panel was dry, he worked on one area at a time—following the method of the tempera painters—first putting in a thin wash of local color and letting the ink drawing show through.

In *The Adoration of the Magi,* which is in the Uffizi Gallery in Florence, it appears that Dürer first painted the black king's head with a transparent burnt umber tone and then added and blended darker burnt umber and black for the shadows. To the light area he added a more opaque brown, composed of white and burnt umber, and blended it in with the shadows, keeping the paint thin and allowing the ink drawing to be revealed slightly. He added the dark accents and details with burnt umber and black, using sable brushes—he kept the colors as thin as watercolor. Finally, he added the highlights of the flesh with an opaque mixture of black and white, which he then blended with a dry brush.

Dürer usually finished each area in one sitting, with the exception of draperies, which he first rendered in black and white and then, in another sitting, glazed over with transparent color.

A strong three-dimensional drawing is a necessity for this technique. Because of this thin, transparent method of working, Dürer's paintings are almost "paintings without paint." There is no real buildup of heavy color. Their brilliance, like that of stained-glass windows, comes from the light within.

COLORS AND BRUSHES

First and second sittings: white lead (flake white), yellow ochre light, Naples yellow, burnt umber, French vermilion light, alizarin crimson, ivory black. Third sitting: white lead, yellow ochre light, Naples yellow, burnt umber, ivory black, Prussian blue.

The brushes I use for all sittings are number 4 round sables, number 6 round bristles, a large flat bristle blender, a ¾″ flat oxhair blender, and a ¼″ flat oxhair blender.

1.
On buff paper I make a precise
drawing from life, using charcoal
and white Conté. I draw it the
exact size needed for the painting
and then trace it on transparent
tracing paper and rub burnt umber pigment on the back. I then
place the drawing on the gesso
panel with the burnt umber side
down.

2.
After tracing the drawing onto the white gesso panel with a sharp instrument, I draw over it with ink. I then brush on a coat of medium tinted with yellow ochre, burnt umber, and a drop of Japan drier to fix the drawing and make the painting surface non-absorbent. Before painting on the panel, I leave it for a few days until it is dry.

3.
Diluting burnt umber with medium, I paint in the face transparently. I then paint the hair with ivory black, the rose with thin white, and the lips with a pink tone.

4.
For the shadows under the chin, in the neck, and where the face turns away from the light, I mix burnt umber with a little ivory black without any medium. With a dry oxhair brush, I blend this mixture into the wet, transparent umber paint.

5.
I now mix a gray made of ivory black and white and model it into the light areas of the flesh—the side of the neck, the upper back, and the sides of the face—blending it into the burnt umber paint.

6.
Using a small sable brush, I now redraw the face with burnt umber and ivory black. I carefully blend in the strokes with a small blender and then begin to add stronger lights on the face and the neck.

7.
I draw in the shadows of the hair with ivory black and blend in a few opaque gray highlights. I then add to the flower a few dark gray accents, some opaque white highlights, and reflections made of yellow ochre and white. I also paint the earrings with yellow ochre and highlight them with a mixture of Naples yellow and white. After working on the head I take a break and begin the second sitting by painting the arm in the same sequence as I painted the head. The first sitting has taken me approximately four hours.

8.
Starting the second sitting, I now model the arm using ivory black for the shadows and shadow accents. When I finish the modeling, I blend the different parts together with a dry brush.

9.
I paint the more opaque light areas with a gray made from ivory black and white. The reflected light on the breast and the forearm are painted with vermilion. I add stronger, lighter gray highlights on the arms, I soften the highlights, and I cover the rest of the body with a thin coat of burnt umber. I then put in the shadows on the rest of the body.

10.
I finish the rest of the body as I did in the earlier stages. As you can see, I start with a base of burnt umber, first putting in the darkest shadows and shadow accents with ivory black and then adding the lighter shadows with gray. I save the strongest lights for the last—they are added in this step. This is the end of the second sitting, which has taken approximately five hours.

11.
I begin the third sitting by mixing on the palette Prussian blue, white, a touch of yellow ochre, and ivory black. I dilute this mixture with medium and start painting the background with a bristle brush.

12.
I finish painting the background and then I blend it with a large dry flat brush. Turning then to the piece of fur that hangs over the woman's shoulder, I paint it with just a thin coat of medium, letting the original ground show through. I then paint in the shadows with burnt umber.

13.
Detail of finished painting. Although the highlights of the face and neck were painted in during step 7, they stand out with more clarity and brilliance once the blue background is completed.

14.
The dark accents of the fur are burnt umber painted in with a small sable brush. The color of the board is used as a middletone for the fur, and I paint in the highlights with a mixture of yellow ochre and white. The bracelet is yellow ochre highlighted with a mixture of Naples yellow and white. This third and final sitting takes approximately two hours.

TECHNIQUES OF
TITIAN

Titian (1485?–1576), the outstanding Venetian painter of his era and one of the greatest influences in painting, developed a new way of working with the Van Eyck oil medium and technique, already shown in the Dürer demonstration. The smooth, lustrous surface of the Van Eyck medium was well suited to the small panel pictures of Northern Europe, but for the large wall paintings of Italy, the glare and reflections became a serious problem. Titian found a vehicle that could easily cover large areas of canvas and dry matte without reflections.

The new medium also allowed greater ease of blending, and Titian was able to create, for the first time, the soft, smokelike edges called *sfumato*. The soft edge created "air" around portraits and figures, setting them into space where they harmonized with the landscape instead of looking as if they had been cut out and pasted on. Titian painted his flesh highlights a cool tone; then, as he painted toward the edges of his figure or portrait, he made shadows and outlines warm and reddish.

MEDIUM

Titian seems to have used a wax-based medium mixed, possibly, with black oil. The medium was probably slow-drying, allowing time to cover large areas and blend them. The wax base enabled him to paint heavy *impastos*—passages of thick paint standing in relief.

He could *glaze* (paint transparently) with his medium or execute *velaturas*—translucent veils of color that allow diffused light to come through the paint. The medium also allowed several coats to be painted on top of each other without cracking.

I use here the same basic demonstration medium that I use in the demonstration of Dürer's technique, but I add beeswax medium to each color and to the basic medium. (Directions for making the beeswax medium can be found on page 17.) I work some of the wax mixture into the jelly medium and place this blend in the center of my palette. The amount of the wax medium you use can vary, depending upon your experience and what works well for you. I use some of this combination of wax and basic medium with each stroke of pigment.

This medium works well and does not become tacky for about four or five hours. You can use linseed oil as an additional diluent if you like. The medium should dry overnight, but it is safest to wait two days between sittings, especially when glazing.

PAINTING SURFACE

Titian's paintings are on canvas, which is a better surface than a wood panel for a technique that requires several sittings. I prefer to paint on a panel because I like the hard surface, so I mount the canvas on a ½″ plywood panel. This gives me my hard surface but is still true to the canvas technique. You may prefer to paint on commercially prepared canvas, and if you do work on this type of surface, be sure to coat it with an extra layer of white lead.

The ground I use for this demonstration, as well as for the demonstrations of the techniques of Veronese and Caravaggio, is one of the safest and probably the oldest. Here is how it is prepared and applied.

1. Prepare rabbit skin glue as described on page 22.

2. When the glue is cool but still liquid, cover the surface of the ½″ plywood with it. Place raw linen canvas on top of the panel and smooth it out with the palm of your hand, letting the edges of the canvas go beyond the edges of the board.

3. Rub jellied glue into the surface of the canvas, smoothing out the glue until the entire surface of the canvas is wet.

4. Turn the board over and apply more jellied glue to adhere the overlapping canvas to the edges and the back of the panel, folding the edges of the fabric.

5. With carpet tacks, small metal tacks, or staples, tack the four folded corners of the canvas to the back of the board.

6. Rub jellied glue into the back of the board to keep it from warping.

7. Turn the board over so the canvas faces up. Use small tacks or staples to attach the canvas around the edges of the board. This will keep the fabric in its place as it dries and shrinks.

8. Scrape off the excess glue with the edge of a palette knife. Then let the panel dry.

9. Sand the surface lightly and paint on a coat of traditional or acrylic gesso. When dry, sand the surface again and then paint another coat on the back of the panel. Repeat this procedure two or three times. If you use the traditional gesso, first dampen the dry gesso before applying the new coat.

10. Paint on a coat of white lead tinted with red ochre or burnt sienna and black to create a warm tone and to make the canvas nonabsorbent. When this is dry, the canvas panel is ready to paint on.

PROBABLE WORKING SEQUENCE

Titian painted his portraits and figures from life and composed his paintings directly on the canvas. The only preliminary drawings he made were landscapes. He used these for reference when he needed a landscape background.

The ground for the painting was usually a warm gray or pinkish color. His first sittings were often painted in red (possibly red ochre or vermilion), black, and white. In Titian's first sittings he probably attacked the canvas with bold strokes, modeling the light forms in gray and painting the shadows and darker tones with warm browns and reds. In the second sitting he would cover the entire flesh area with a *velatura* of gray and start to refine and blend the forms. In additional sittings he would cover the flesh area with *velaturas* of flesh tones and finally work up to a full-color range.

A description of Titian's late style by Palma il Giovanni (1544–1628) indicates that he disregarded contours and constructed his composition in large areas of flat color, letting the edges overlap and blend together. This allowed him to alter his composition and make other changes very easily. Then he would turn the canvas to the wall to dry. After a period of time—days, weeks, or even months—he would turn the canvas around, stare at it critically, and begin again. Thus, by repeated revisions, glazes, and *velaturas,* he would perfect his pictures, painting his final stages more with his fingers than with a brush. Because of this working procedure, he always had several paintings going at once. He obviously never painted *alla prima*—that is, in one continuous operation.

COLORS AND BRUSHES

Nude. First sitting: white lead (flake white), burnt umber, ivory black. Second sitting: white lead, yellow ochre light, burnt sienna, burnt umber, ivory black. Third sitting: white lead, chrome yellow, Naples yellow, French vermilion light, alizarin crimson, burnt umber, ivory black, ultramarine blue.

Portrait. First and third sittings: white lead (flake white), yellow ochre light, burnt sienna, burnt umber, ivory black. Second sitting: white lead, Naples yellow, French vermilion light, alizarin crimson, burnt umber, ivory black. Fourth sitting: same as second sitting with addition of chrome yellow, Prussian blue, ultramarine blue. Fifth and sixth sittings: white lead, yellow ochre light, French vermilion light, alizarin crimson, burnt umber, ivory black.

My brushes are numbers 4, 5, 6, 7, 8, and 11 round bristles, number 6 round sables, and large flat bristle blenders.

DEMONSTRATION ONE

1.
Painting from life, I paint an outline of the nude on canvas, using a mixture of burnt umber and medium.

2.
I cover the areas that will be flesh with a light gray tone made of ivory black and white. Then I draw in shadows with a darker gray. Most of these darker tones are shadow accents.

3.
Following the contours of the forms, I now mark pure white highlights into the light gray flesh tone. These are the points at which the strongest light hits the form.

4.
With a large flat bristle blender, I blend the white highlights into the underlying tone. No real work has been done yet on the hair, so I now fill in this area with a flat burnt umber tone. I then define the figure more fully with burnt umber accents and various shades of gray made from ivory black and white. I also continue to blend the flesh tones.

5.
I define the face more and model the rest of the body, softening the edges of the forms with a blender. This first sitting takes approximately four hours. I leave the painting to dry, hoping that it will be dry enough for a second sitting the next day.

6.
I begin the second sitting. I add medium to a gray middletone to create a mixture that is called a *halfpaste*. This is a translucent color made by diluting opaque paint with medium. I now paint this halfpaste over the entire body surface, letting the underpainting show through. I then blend the halfpaste and add more pure white highlights. I model these into the underlying tone to bring the existing tone up to a higher key. I then turn to the drapery and start with white for the light areas and gray for the shadows and folds.

7.
To finish the drapery, I paint in the light areas with white and the shadow areas with gray. I then turn to the surrounding objects and render them in combinations of burnt umber, burnt sienna, yellow ochre and gray. I keep all my paint thin by brush pressure rather than by diluting the paint with medium.

8.
I do a lot of work in the background at this point, painting with grays and burnt umber, which I apply thinly, as if working with watercolor. You can see that a great deal of detail is added in the background. However, I have not yet gotten to any real variety in color. I continue to use my simple umbers and grays, as I am still working in the underpainting stage. I leave the painting to dry until the next day. This second sitting takes approximately four hours.

9.
Because the figure and the background are not yet dry enough to paint on, I turn to the still life in the third sitting. Using a full palette of colors, I paint the fruit *alla prima.* I make my greens with ivory black and chrome yellow light, or with Prussian blue and one of the yellows plus white. I also paint in the landscape seen through the window, again using a full palette of colors. The approximate time of this third sitting is three hours.

10.
I begin the fourth sitting. Making a flesh tone of yellow ochre, French vermilion, and medium into a halfpaste, I paint over the figure with paint thin enough to let the gray underpainting show through. I leave the face and one arm untouched, but I add vermilion touches to various parts of the body where I will want stronger color.

11.
With a dry brush, I now blend the flesh tones that I put down in step 11. I then add opaque highlights of yellow ochre and white, and vermilion and white. Notice how the firm, solid strokes of the highlights follow the forms.

12.
I now blend and drybrush these tones into each other. Then, using vermilion and burnt umber, which I apply with a sable brush, I reestablish details in the toes and fingers. In this step you can see clearly the two highlight mixtures described in step 11.

13.
I continue to blend the flesh tones, which gradually become more smooth and more luminous. The face and one arm are still untouched. The gray underpainting is still exposed.

14.
Using small sable brushes, I paint the face and hand the same way I painted the rest of the body. I sharpen the details of the face with small strokes and accentuate the darks, the highlights, and the warm colors.

15.
Using a mixture of burnt sienna and medium applied with a small sable brush, I paint over the hair and then add shadows to it with burnt umber. I paint in the highlights of the hair using yellow ochre and white, making my strokes follow the forms of the curls in the hair. Then I turn to the curtain in the background, using a mixture of Prussian blue and ivory black. Finally, I render the guitar with burnt umber, gray, and ivory black. I render the pillows and the red drapery with thin *velaturas*—semitransparent layers—of colors and grays accented with opaque white highlights. I glaze the lower corners of the painting with a mixture of black and medium.

16.
I now paint in the details of the red drapery at the sitter's feet, using the tip of a small sable brush. This is the end of the fourth sitting, which takes approximately six hours.

17.
In the fifth and sixth sittings I rework the body, following a procedure similar to steps 11, 12, and 13. I paint in and blend a final halfpaste of middletone flesh colors, and then once again work in opaque whites and soften them. Then I paint in the highlights of the curtain with a mixture of white, Prussian blue, and ivory black, blending in all these. I apply a wet coat of medium to the areas where details are to be painted in, and then I put in details of the book and pillows and make final touch-ups. In the finished painting, the tone of the body is smoother, simpler, and more luminous. It is also more unified.

DEMONSTRATION TWO

1.
Painting directly from life, I rough in the outline of the portrait and paint in the dark areas with burnt umber and medium.

2.
With a gray tone made of ivory black and white I paint in the light areas of the flesh. I then paint in the light section of the dress with white and the shadow section with gray.

3.
I now paint in the darker shadow areas with a darker gray than I used in Step 2. You can see these darker tones on the forehead, eye-sockets, cheek, jaw, and breast.

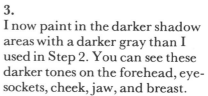

4.
Using burnt umber, I restate the features. Then with a flat coat of burnt sienna diluted with medium, I paint in the hair. I add shadow accents with a mixture of burnt umber and ivory black. You can see these accents along the chin, on the cheek bone, and in the shadow cast by the lock of hair falling over the eye.

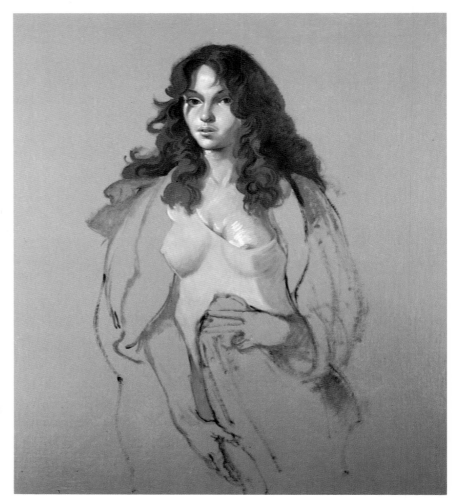

5.
Using brushstrokes that follow the form, I paint in pure white highlights on the breast and in areas of the face. Using a dry brush, I then blend these lights into the wet underlying color.

6.
Now, using a pure heavy white, I draw in the highlights of the dress; with a darker gray I paint in the folds that form the shadows. This combination of white in the highlights and gray in the folds creates the look of soft fabric clinging to the sitter's body. I then paint in the arm with a medium gray.

7.
Here I render the arms and hands more fully, following the same procedure I used in painting the head. I also blend and soften the tones of the neck and breast.

8.
With a mixture of burnt umber, ivory black, and medium, I now paint in the dark shadows of the robe.

9.
Using a mixture of yellow ochre and burnt umber, I scrub in the light section of the robe. Adding this color gives the fabric texture and body. I will gradually refine the robe by adding highlights and shadow accents. I also start the background here with a mixture of yellow ochre and ivory black.

10.
I complete the background and blend it with a large, flat bristle brush. Then with yellow ochre, I paint stronger lights on the robe and work them into the still-wet color beneath. I also redefine the shadows with burnt umber. I then place opaque highlights in the hair with yellow ochre and white.

11.
I finish and refine the features of the face, working with sable brushes and burnt umber for the dark shadows, and gray and white for the lighter tones. I also correct the sides of the hands. This is the end of the first sitting.

12.
I begin the second sitting by brushing a thin glaze of vermilion over the lower part of the background and the robe and around the figure. Some of the glaze spills over the edges of the robe.

13.
I blend the background with a dry brush. Now the dark edges of the robe seem to melt softly into the background. I then paint the design on the robe using Naples yellow in the light area and yellow ochre in the shadow.

14.
I finish the design in the robe and add a flesh tone—a mixture of yellow ochre, French vermilion, and medium—over the light areas of the flesh. I add touches of the vermilion to the cheeks and lips for color. I also add this vermilion to the gray shadow areas on the flesh to create reflected light and to give the form roundness.

15.
With a dry blending brush, I now blend together the flesh tones and the vermilion that I put down in step 14. You can see that the gray underpainting still shows through.

16.
Trying to get the form of the face complete, I model in opaque highlights of yellow ochre and white. I now begin work on the arms in the same way I painted the face. As you can see, I start with a gray underpainting and add darker grays and white highlights. I add flesh tones made of a mixture of yellow ochre, vermilion, and medium, and then paint in a few strokes of pure vermilion.

17.
I blend and lighten the tones on the arms and hands, softly merging the warm strokes of step 16 with the lighter tones.

18.
I now boldly mark in highlights of yellow ochre and white on the right arm and then blend them with a dry blending brush.

19.
At this final stage I finish the arms by blending the tones softly together. Notice how the edges of the forearm blur delicately into the surrounding shadow tones. With small brushes I paint in the last details such as the ring and the ribbon.

TECHNIQUES OF
VERONESE

Paolo Veronese (1528–1588) was born in Verona but later on settled in Venice. He was one of the great colorists of all time. Unlike Titian and Tintoretto, who subdued their color for *chiaroscuro*—strong contrasts of light and shadow—Veronese never allowed color to become secondary. He thought of his canvas as a tapestry of interwoven colors.

Veronese's paintings are opaque, with even the shadows painted in color. Because his large, decorative canvases were usually hung in big, dark interiors, he avoided black shadows (like those in Tintoretto's paintings) and wanted his work to be bright. Veronese also painted in fresco, an opaque technique in which the shadows are made colorful in order to give them life. It is possible that to achieve both these effects he went in the direction of full color, harmonizing warm colors against cool colors in such a way that even his neutral or earth colors seem to take on a tint, and the whole painting vibrates.

MEDIUM

Veronese probably painted with the same medium used by Titian and Tintoretto—one containing beeswax and possibly black oil. He often used *impasto* brushstrokes and painted both light and shadows opaquely.

For my demonstration I work with the same combination of the basic medium and beeswax medium that I use in the Titian demonstration. Recipes for these mediums can be found on pages 13 and 17. I work some of the wax mixture into each color on my palette. I also work some of it into the jelly medium and place this blend in the center of my palette. Remember that this medium does not become tacky for about four or five hours. It probably will not be dry enough to paint on the next day, so skip a day before beginning your next sitting.

PAINTING SURFACE

Veronese painted on canvas, usually tinted a tone of gray. The weave of the canvas is large, and many of his canvases seem rather thinly coated with white lead or gesso. Since in the large paintings he was after a matte finish without glare, he may have prepared the canvas this way to retain a slightly absorbent ground.

Here again my painting surface is canvas mounted on plywood panel and prepared in the manner described in the Titian demonstration on page 41.

PROBABLE WORKING SEQUENCE

Veronese was not a portrait painter, but he painted large figure compositions in which he incorporated many heads. After making a drawing from life, he would copy it freehand on his canvas, painting in a warm brown tone. In this part of his first sitting he would work to establish the composition and drawing. He would then work in his light tones with a warm gray mixed from white and his original brown.

He began his second sitting by painting the flesh, drapery, and background in flat tones; at this stage he applied his paint so thinly that the dry underpainting could still be seen. Into the flesh he would work variations of the flesh tones, plus light and dark tones, modeling until the forms were round. In the draperies he would often mark only the highlights and not paint in the shadows at all, using only two tones—middle value and highlight.

After everything was done, he might devote a final sitting to putting in dark glazes, possibly to strengthen a shadow area or soften contours. Veronese used his paint heavily, seldom blending, and achieved most of his effects in two or three sittings. His canvases are all matte and opaque. Their vibrancy comes from the juxtaposition of colors.

COLORS AND BRUSHES

First sitting: white lead (flake white), raw umber. Second sitting: white lead, yellow ochre light, chrome yellow, French vermilion light, alizarin crimson, burnt umber, ivory black, ultramarine blue. Third sitting: ivory black.

For the first and second sitting I use numbers 4, 5, 6, 7, and 11 round bristle brushes. In the third sitting I add a large flat bristle blender.

1.
I begin by making a drawing from life on buff paper using charcoal, red chalk, and white Conté.

2.
I rough in the position of the figure on the canvas with raw umber mixed with a little medium. I use a round bristle brush.

3.
I now paint in the shadows using the same color and brush as I used in step 2. These dark flat shadow areas begin to define the form, giving it contour, and are the basis for later, lighter shadows, which will go on top of them.

4.
Using various neutral shades made of raw umber and white diluted with medium, I paint in different areas of the form as well as the clothing. I reserve pure, dark, raw umber for the shadow areas.

5.
Into the middletone of the flesh I now mark stronger lights using white medium. I also improve the drawing by painting first with my dark value and then with my light, overlapping the tones and correcting each time. I then paint in final heavy *impastos* for the highlights. This first sitting takes approximately five hours.

6.
In the second sitting, I add medium to yellow ochre and French vermilion to make a halfpaste. I then paint the halfpaste over the dry underpainting of the face and hand.

7.
For red color I add tints of vermilion for the nose, cheeks, knuckles, and fingers. These will be blended later. Notice also that some of these will be covered later by white highlights.

8.
I now blend the flesh tones to-gether with a large, dry, flat blender. I then paint a glaze of burnt umber and medium over the hair and beard and blend it in with a dry brush.

9.
Using a mixture of yellow ochre and burnt umber, I paint in the opaque highlights of the hair. These highlights are modeled into the wet umber that I put on the hair in step 8. I am using the same brush that I worked with in step 8. I then paint in the shadows of the hair with ivory black.

10.
Now I paint even stronger highlights into the hair, using a sable brush and a gray that is a mixture of ivory black and white. Notice how the strokes follow the direction of the hair. I also give further definition to the eyes and mouth with burnt umber.

11.
I also paint back into the flesh with stronger lights. You can see these particularly above the eyebrow and in the forehead. I blend the edges of the strokes into the wet undercoat of paint and then touch up and finish the dark details of the face.

12.
Using an even lighter mixture of white and yellow ochre, I mark in the highlight areas with heavy *impasto* and leave them unblended.

13.
I glaze in ultramarine blue for the jacket, leaving the lower part of the jacket arm unglazed for the moment.

14.
I now finish applying the blue glaze for the jacket. I blend the glaze and then paint in opaque highlights using a mixture of white, ultramarine blue, and ivory black. I use heavy paint for these highlights and blend the edges of the strokes into the wet glaze I put down in step 13.

15.
I finish the jacket using basically only two tones—highlights and middletones—in the creases of the jacket and where the folds catch the light at the top. These tones give the jacket contour and make it fit the body. I paint in the shirt with pure white adding dark gray accents. On the palette I mix yellow ochre, white, and ivory black; then, returning to the canvas, I paint the background with this mixture. This second sitting takes approximately five hours.

16.
In the third and final sitting, I now glaze the lower corners of the painting with
a thin mixture of ivory black and medium, blending it after I finish laying it on.
I also glaze in the shadows on the inside of the right arm in the same way. I
paint this thin glaze over the eye sockets, then blend it in. These final glazes
take about one-half hour to execute.

TECHNIQUES OF
CARAVAGGIO

Michelangelo Caravaggio (1573–1610) was born near Milan and studied with Simone Peterzano, who probably had been a student of Titian. In his early still-life paintings Caravaggio developed a style of strong *chiaroscuro*—strong contrast between areas of dark and light—which was to become his trademark. Not only was his dramatic *chiaroscuro* style novel, but his use of peasant types and contemporary costumes was also regarded as revolutionary. He rejected idealized saints and Madonnas and developed a vividly realistic style.

Caravaggio, like Titian, seems to have worked directly on the canvas without the usual preparatory drawings. But this is a debatable point, since no Caravaggio drawings exist; it *is* possible that he used drawings, tracing them and then destroying them after they were used. I believe this is probably because his compositions are carefully planned, and the shadow areas reveal most of the underlying ground color—if he had painted from life, he would have made many changes, and the ground would have become muddy. Here I work from a drawing.

Caravaggio's dark, almost black, shadows and his theatrical effects started a whole school of imitators. His work influenced Rubens, Velasquez, and Rembrandt.

MEDIUM

Caravaggio's medium must have been similar to Titian's. My medium for this demonstration is the same one I use in the demonstration showing Titian's and Veronese's techniques: a combination of the basic medium and the beeswax medium. I mix a little of the beeswax medium with each tube color on my palette and with the basic jelly medium. I place a small amount of the jelly-wax combination in the center of my palette to be used as I paint. Recipes for these mediums can be found on pages 13 and 17.

PAINTING SURFACE

Caravaggio's paintings are on canvas similar to that used by Titian but darker in tone. He used this tone—almost unpainted—for his shadow effects. For this demonstration I use the same type of surface that I use for the Titian demonstration—canvas mounted on a ½″ wood panel. Refer to the Titian demonstration for directions on how to prepare this painting surface. You can also use commercially prepared canvas, but be sure to give it an extra coat of white lead.

PROBABLE WORKING SEQUENCE

It is not known whether Caravaggio began his paintings from life or from a drawing. His first sitting was probably rendered completely with warm, thin color, possibly burnt umber, which he handled like watercolor, leaving the color of the ground untouched for the lighter areas and painting the shadows with transparent color diluted with medium. The underlying tone of the canvas would show through the shadows. There is no buildup of paint from any of the first sitting, which indicates that the tones were well blended.

In the second sitting he would work into the flesh tones with shades of opaque grays and then model and blend them into the shadow edges, being careful not to paint back into the shadow itself. The second sitting would look a great deal like Titian's second sitting, but there would be no buildup of lights. The shadows would be translucent, and all the inner forms would be well blended.

In the third sitting Caravaggio would paint *velaturas* of flesh tints over the gray underpainting. He would work subtle grays and pinks into the shadow areas for reflected lights. The fourth sitting would be reserved for details, more subtle glazes, and tints. The final sitting would be for large overall dark glazes in which he could manipulate the shadows and control the lights.

COLORS AND BRUSHES

First sitting: burnt umber. Second sitting: white lead (flake white), burnt umber, ivory black. Third and fourth sittings: white lead, yellow ochre light, French vermilion light, alizarin crimson, burnt sienna, burnt umber, ivory black. Fifth sitting: ivory black.

My brushes are numbers 4, 5, 6, 8, 9, and 11 round bristles, number 6 round sables, and flat bristle blenders.

1.
There are no traces of Caravaggio's drawings. He could have painted directly from life; but more than likely he did do a preliminary drawing, and after transferring or copying it, he destroyed it. The sole purpose of the drawing was a plan for the painting. I do my drawing from life with charcoal, red Conté, and white Conté on buff paper.

2.
I copy the drawing, which is the exact size needed for the painting, onto the dark-toned canvas with burnt umber diluted with medium. I paint in some of the flat shadow areas, keeping these shadows transparent and letting the color of the ground show through.

3.
I now render the figure more fully with burnt umber and medium. I brush in more shadows with the burnt umber and medium and outline sharp edges, such as the outside edge of the right arm and the edge of the forearm, and up into the fingers. I also begin painting in the background, using a dark umber glaze.

4.
I finish the painting completely in umber tones, keeping the paint thin to give it a washlike effect. I also finish the background in dark umber tones. This ends the first setting.

5.
I begin the second sitting by mixing neutral tones of burnt umber and white to paint into the light areas of the face. I paint in the beard with a flat middletone of gray made from ivory black and white.

6.
Adding black to the neutral mixture I used in step 5, I make a dark gray, which I paint into shadow areas such as the temple and around the white highlights below the eye. I blend this gray with a dry brush.

7.
I now use pure white highlights to model forms in the face. I paint the flat shadow side of the beard with a medium dark gray. Then, using a thin gray diluted with medium, I carefully paint reflected light into the shadow side of the face and the beard. Notice that I let some of the brown underpainting show through on the flesh.

8.
I begin to render the sitter's right arm, which is in the light, as well as the chest in the same manner as I did the head. I use neutral tones of burnt umber and white and flat gray tones of ivory black and white. I place white areas along the outside of the of the sitter's right forearm, the wrist, and up around the right shoulder area. I then model darker shadows into the upper arm and down into the chest. I also paint dark shadows in the recesses of the collarbone on the sitter's left side. I start painting in the neutral middletone—made from burnt umber and white—on the sitter's left shoulder and the shadow accents on the sitter's left collarbone.

9.
I highlight the beard, using pure white, and then go on to finish the rest of the body with neutrals made from burnt umber and white. Then, with a gray made from ivory black and white, I also render in the books immediately around the sitter and the papers he is reading.

10.
I finally finish the *grisaille* (gray) underpainting of the books, but I leave the shadows and the background a transparent burnt umber. This is the end of the second sitting.

11.
I now begin the third sitting. I paint the drapery using a mixture of French vermilion and burnt sienna for the base color and I work in the shadows with burnt umber and ivory black. I then paint in the highlights with yellow ochre and vermilion and blend them with a dry brush. I go back to the body and mix a flesh-color *velatura* of yellow ochre and vermilion, which I paint all over the torso.

12.
I begin to add stronger lights on the chest and arm and boldly mark in highlights with yellow ochre and white.

13.
On the top of the flesh color I now stroke pure vermilion flesh tints on the shoulders and the knuckles. I drybrush and blend the torso and the arms.

14.
I again blend the torso and work in stronger lights. I put a flesh tone of yellow ochre and vermilion over the light part of the face, applying the paint thinly enough to let the underpainting show through.

15.
Once again I put in vermilion touches, this time on the nose and cheeks. Then on the forehead and nose I mark in highlights with yellow ochre and white.

16.
I soften various tones of the face, carefully blending the edges of the forms without losing their shapes. Since I have done so much work to model the face and to get the flesh tones right, I must now sharpen the details of the face with burnt umber and ivory black, which I apply with a small sable brush. I also paint in the glazes on the hair and chest, again using a small brush. This is the end of the third sitting.

17.
I now begin the fourth sitting. Using two small sable brushes, I paint in the details of the books and the chair. I use one brush for the shadows, which I make with burnt umber diluted with medium, and the other for the highlights, which I make with white, yellow ochre, and ivory black.

18.
I now glaze the drapery with burnt sienna and alizarin crimson thinned with medium. I then paint and blend highlights made with vermilion and burnt sienna into the wet glaze. Then I finish the chair, painting in the cane back, completing the carved sections, and placing in the highlights. This is the end of the fourth sitting.

19.
I begin the fifth sitting by glazing the background with a mixture of ivory black and medium. I then blend it with a large, flat, dry bristle brush. Some of the glaze overlaps the chair and so helps to create atmosphere. At this point I also put in the pictures in the pages of the book and the papers the sitter is reading.

20.
Using a thin glaze of ivory black and medium, I finish the leg of the table and the two lower corners of the painting and then blend in this glaze. I also glaze the background with the same mixture and blend it in. The smoother tone of the background is less distracting and emphasizes the dramatic lighting on the figure, which stands out in bold relief.

TECHNIQUES OF
RUBENS

Peter Paul Rubens (1577–1640), the greatest baroque painter, possessed the most versatile painting medium that any artist has ever used. His technique was ideal for free, rapid work, and his output was enormous. His range of subject matter seems limitless; and huge commissions or canvases did not deter him. Rubens's style has had unending influence on artists throughout history, from great contemporaries like Van Dyck and Jordaens to later masters like Watteau, Delacroix, and Renoir.

He studied in Italy for nine years, where he became impressed with the grandiose style of the Italian painters, as well as their use of a medium that could cover large surfaces. While working on his own paintings, he also copied the masters and was especially attracted to the canvases of Titian. Throughout his career Rubens continued copying to improve his facility. Even as a mature artist, he copied twenty-one Titians, nine Raphaels, and, on a diplomatic mission to Spain, a Tintoretto.

In Titian's work Rubens admired the flesh tones and particularly the soft edges—called *sfumato* in Italian—which Titian achieved by executing a series of *velaturas* (translucent or semitransparent paint layers) and transparent glazes. Titian painted over a *grisaille* underpainting, which was actually a fully developed picture in tones of gray. Rubens wanted to achieve the same results, but he wanted to do it *alla prima*—to paint directly in one continuous operation.

The technique that Rubens searched for and found was a combination of the brilliant Flemish technique (exemplified by Dürer) and the broad Italian style (exemplified by Titian). But the matte Italian surface restricted the range and brilliance of his colors, while playing down the variations between thick and thin paint. Rubens needed a medium that would produce the lustrous surface necessary to make his transparencies effective. What he found was a medium that made his paint rich and luminous, allowing him to work with a maximum of contrast. He played thin, transparent passages against thick, opaque areas; light against shadow; strong brushstrokes against blended *sfumato* edges; cool colors against warm; and dark colors against light.

MEDIUM

Rubens's medium seems to have been a thick jelly, glowing and transparent, that retained the shape and texture of his brushstroke, both in the darks and in the lights. It was liquid enough to cover large areas but set up fast enough not to run. It held firm enough for drybrush effects and allowed him to blend colors into one another without making them muddy. The medium allowed a black line to be drawn through a patch of wet white without going gray, and vice versa.

The only drawback to his medium was that it set up quickly and thus became too tacky to work with after a few hours. Lesser artists than Rubens, without his unerring drawing, had trouble handling it. But for Rubens it was the perfect medium and suited his flamboyant *alla prima* style.

For this demonstration I use the variation of the basic medium. You can find the recipe for it on page 14. The variation calls for considerably less linseed oil and more mastic tears than does the basic medium. These proportions result in a medium that is much thicker, though still a jelly like the basic medium. It also becomes tacky much faster. I like this medium because it suits my rapid painting method and it is sure to dry overnight. But you will have to experiment with it. If you find that it is too thick and becomes tacky too soon, you can thin it with linseed oil to slow the drying time.

PAINTING SURFACE

Rubens preferred a white panel streaked with a thin warm umber tone to canvas because the panel reflected more light. Rubens liked these striations because they would show through the large transparent shadow areas, breaking up the reflected light and making the whole passage vibrate. The warm undertone had to be dry and nonabsorbent before Rubens started painting so that the tone would not be dissolved by subsequent layers of paint.

In the two demonstrations that follow I use ¼" untempered Masonite. Well-seasoned wood is even better, but it is difficult to find. Obviously, Rubens never used the modern gesso I suggest, but it is a good substitute for his painting surface. Here is how to prepare the surface.

1. Give the smooth side of the Masonite one coat of acrylic gesso, using a large flat brush. Then apply the gesso to the rough side to prevent warping.

2. When the panel is dry, sand it slightly and then repeat the application of the gesso, again sanding lightly between applications. Remember to cover both sides of the panel.

3. Tint a 50–50 mixture of acrylic matte medium and water with burnt umber—powdered pigment, acrylic, or watercolor. Apply this final isolating coat with a large brush, leaving the brush striations on the panel.

4. When the panel is dry, it is ready for use.

PROBABLE WORKING SEQUENCE

Rubens seldom painted from life. He nearly always used a very complete drawing in which he had already solved all the problems of composition and drawing. Thus, when he started to paint, he was not burdened by the model and could concentrate solely on applying the paint.

He first sketched the portrait or figure on the panel with a thin wash of color—as liquid as a watercolor wash—using a warm brown tone to indicate the shadow areas. An outline indicated the light area. Then a translucent middletone (for flesh) was laid over the light area. Color was added to such areas as red cheeks and lips. The light and shadow areas were almost the same value—except that one was transparent and the other translucent; and they could be modeled together until the form was correct.

Various grays, which were simple mixtures of black and white, were then applied to make the transitions between light and shadow. The grays were also used for shadows on the light side of the form—shadows that were not dark enough to be in burnt umber. Rubens also used these grays to make forms recede. Since stronger colors appear to come forward, the grays seem to fall back. If there was a "secret" to Rubens's color combinations, it certainly must have been his cool grays. When used next to the pink flesh tones, these grays take on a blue or even green hue.

Once the gray was modeled into the form, reflected lights were painted into the transparent shadows with reds or grays. Up until this point the portrait or figure had to be kept in a low key. Now came the final two stages: application of first the light and then the shadow accents. The light tones were heavy and opaque; the highlight on the flesh was never white alone but always mixed with some flesh tone. Shadow accents were marked in with dark burnt umber, crimson, or black. The paint was then softened or given further accents where needed.

Rubens's technique required more courage than that of other painters because of the unfinished appearance of each stage. Only at the end does the painting pull together. By this direct approach Rubens was able to paint a fully rendered three-dimensional head in just a few hours.

COLORS AND BRUSHES

Portrait. These are the colors I use in the order I place them on my palette: white lead (flake white), Naples yellow, yellow ochre light, French vermilion light, alizarin crimson, burnt sienna, burnt umber, ivory black, ultramarine blue.

My brushes are numbers 4, 5, and 8 round bristles, number 4 round sables, and large flat bristle blenders.

Nude. I use the same palette for the figure demonstration, substituting Prussian blue for the ultramarine blue of my portrait palette.

My brushes are numbers 6 and 8 round bristles, number 4 round sables, large flat bristle blenders, and ½″ flat oxhair blenders.

1.
I make a finished drawing from
life on buff paper with black chalk
or charcoal, red chalk, and white
Conté. I use red for tints of warm
color and white for highlights and
light areas. The color of the paper
serves for halftones and reflected
lights. The direction of the line
follows the form.

2.
I lay in the portrait on the panel with a bristle brush and a small amount of medium tinted with burnt umber, giving careful attention to proportion and composition. Details are unimportant at this stage. Corrections can easily be made by wiping off the strokes with a cloth and then repainting.

3.
Using the same brush I used in step 2, I scrub in the hair with burnt sienna diluted with a small amount of medium. Note that some medium should be blended into each color mixture, but the amount of medium should be very small. Only practice will tell you how much to use. One obvious sign of *too* much is that the painting surface becomes slippery. Here I also paint in some of the background, using a combination of ivory black, white, and ultramarine blue. Keeping my paint thin, I mix the colors directly on the panel and work them into each other.

4.
I paint in the dark parts of the hair with burnt umber. I keep these shadow areas transparent, however, so that the light of the board shows through.

5.
I paint in the highlights of the hair with Naples yellow applied with a clean sable brush. The strokes of the highlights follow the contours of the hair, and I blend the ends of these strokes into the underlying color, leaving the centers of the highlights thick and untouched. I am careful to keep the opaque Naples yellow out of the transparent shadows.

6.
I mix a gray from ivory black and white and paint in the shadow areas of the face, neck, and breast, keeping the paint thin and translucent. I also paint in the gray wherever a form turns and recedes, such as at the outside edge of the cheek and on the breast. A separate bristle brush is used for each color.

7.
Using yellow ochre, white, and French vermilion, I make a middletone for the flesh, which I paint into the light areas of the face and breast. This tone should overlap all the edges, leaving none of the bare board showing. I then brush additional touches of the vermilion into areas that have a pink tone: eyelids, cheeks, nose, and mouth.

8.
Drawing into the existing wet paint with burnt umber, I sharpen the drawing of the head and features.

9.
I blend the colors into each other with a large, dry bristle brush, working first in one direction and then in the opposite. I only want to soften the colors, not change the existing shapes. I then improve upon the drawing of the portrait, restating and correcting with each of the basic values—flesh tone, gray, and burnt umber—using a separate brush for each color. I paint in reflections under the nose and chin with vermilion.

10.
For highlights I mix a lighter flesh tone of white and yellow ochre. Working with this lighter tone—quite heavy and opaque because of the texture of the white lead paint—I then mark in the highlights. I am careful not to add too much light to the skin tone. Remember that no pure white is visible in the living subject.

11.
Using separate bristle brushes for each color, I model the head more finely. I work the brushes back and forth from light to shadow as I make corrections with each stroke.

12.
I now restate highlights, soften edges, and paint final details. I also mark in the deep accents of the nostril and the line between the lips. The highlights are not pure white but have some flesh color in them. I start the hands with the same procedure I used in the head.

13.
I finish the hands in the same sequence of steps I used for painting the face. Then I paint in the coat with a transparent mixture of burnt umber and ivory black.

14.
I paint in the background with a mixture of white, ivory black, ultramarine blue, and a little medium. If the color is too dark or too light, it can be corrected by adding more color directly to the panel and then working it in with a brush until the tone is right. The edges of the hair and the coat are overlapped by the blue, so there is no hard line. If too much of the hair or the jacket shape is lost in the overlapping, the form can be restated with dark paint. It is important to "fill" shapes with color and not have hard lines or bare spaces between the background and the figure. The soft edges—the *sfumato*—give a feeling of air and space around the subject.

15.
I use a gray made of black and white to draw the highlights of the jacket and then use the black alone for the dark accents of the folds.

16.
I paint in the shirt with pure white, pressing hard on my brush to produce a thin layer of paint. I then use a mixture of yellow ochre and burnt umber for the flat tone of the pants and a mixture of alizarin crimson and ivory black for the scarf.

17.
I model the shirt with gray for the shadows and then paint in the shadow areas of the scarf and pants with burnt umber and ivory black.

18.
I put in the highlights of the shirt with a heavy, pure white and then soften their edges. For highlights on the pants, I mix yellow ochre, white, and burnt umber. I then mix vermilion with alizarin and ivory black for the highlights of the scarf.

19.
Detail of finished painting.

20.
I paint in details such as the rings and other small touch-ups to finish the portrait. Working *alla prima* I complete the painting in approximately six hours.

DEMONSTRATION TWO

1.
I make a drawing from life on buff paper, using charcoal, white Conté, and touches of red Conté.

2.
On the panel I rough in the figure with a little medium tinted with burnt umber.

3.
I scrub in the hair with a thin coat of transparent burnt sienna and then paint in the shadows of the hair with a transparent mixture of burnt umber and ivory black. I then use a mixture of yellow ochre and ivory black diluted with medium for the background around the head, overlapping the edges between the hair and the background to keep them soft.

4.
I paint in an opaque gray made from black and white for the highlights of the hair. The highlight strokes follow the form of the hair, and I blend the ends of the strokes into the underlying color. I then paint a thinner gray on the face.

5.
The colors surrounding the head, which I put down in step 3, help me to judge the proper flesh tone to mix now that I begin painting the face. I mix a middletone of white, yellow ochre, and French vermilion. I dilute the mixture with a little medium and apply it thinly to a light area of the face. The thinness comes from the pressure of the brush, not from adding a lot of medium. Too much medium will make the panel slippery. I brush pure vermilion into areas that have a pink tone, such as eyelids, cheeks, nose, mouth, and chin. It is wise to begin with strong colors because these colors lose their power as the paint is modeled.

6.
I correct the drawing of the head with burnt umber and paint in dark accents with alizarin crimson and medium. I then mix two different highlight tones on the palette with separate brushes, one with yellow ochre and white, and the other with vermilion and white. I use the highlight made of yellow ochre and white for the forehead, nose, and chin; I use the vermilion highlight wherever there are pink tones.

7.
I now model the head more precisely, moving any bristle brushes back and forth from light to shadow, softening edges. I do the final softening with a small oxhair blender. I extend the background, creating variations by mixing colors directly on the panel and not on the palette. I then paint in thin, flat tones for the pillows and add black for the shadows. The pillow closest to the sitter's shoulder is a mixture of alizarin crimson and burnt umber. The little pillow is yellow ochre and burnt umber. The pillow by the sitter's leg is a combination of alizarin crimson and Prussian blue. I begin to paint in the shirt over the shoulder with a gray made of black and white.

8.
I paint in the shadows of the shirt with a gray darker than the tone I started with in step 8. I paint in the shadows of the pillows with burnt umber and black. For the highlights on the pillows, I use a mixture of white and each pillow color. I also paint in a fourth pillow using alizarin crimson and burnt umber, and the fifth pillow on the end using yellow ochre and burnt umber.

9.
I start the torso and arm the same way I started the head, first painting in gray tones for the receding planes and for the transitional tones between shadow and light, then strengthening the shadows with burnt umber. I paint pure white into the shirt at this point.

10.
I now paint a middle flesh tone into the light areas of the torso, using a mixture of yellow ochre, vermilion, and white. I overlap and model this tone into the surrounding grays and umber. On the arm and hand I also stroke in some pure vermilion.

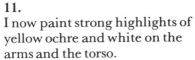

11.
I now paint strong highlights of yellow ochre and white on the arms and the torso.

12.
I blend in the highlights I put down in step 12 and also blend all the inner forms of the torso, keeping the edges of the forms soft. I keep the contrast of the hand against the breast strong to make the hand come forward. This rendering of the hand in front of the breast shows three kinds of contrast: transparent shadow against opaque light; dark against light; and sharp edge with soft edge.

13.
I paint in the legs, feet, and other arm in the same manner as I did the rest of the body. I then finish the shirt by adding heavy, pure white highlights and then softening the edges.

14.
Using a thin mixture of yellow ochre, burnt umber, and a little black, I paint in the floor. I then paint the table with a transparent wash of burnt umber diluted with medium, placing the dark shadow accents with black.

15.
I now paint and blend opaque highlights into the table. I paint in the design of the rug rather freely and impressionistically.

16.
I blend the design of the rug with a large, dry bristle blender and paint in a flat tone of Prussian blue and black for the couch.

17.
On the right side of the couch I paint in shadows, using black. On the left side of the couch, where the subject is sitting, I add and blend in highlights made of white mixed with Prussian blue.

18.
I finish the couch and soften all the edges.

19.
I add the flowers and the vase to the wet background, using yellow ochre and
Prussian blue for the leaves, and white, vermilion, and alizarin crimson for the
roses. I suggest the vase with white highlights and a few touches of gray and
black. I add the final designs on the pillows. I have executed this demonstration
alla prima in approximately nine hours.

TECHNIQUES OF
HALS

Frans Hals (1580?–1666), famous for his bravado technique and lifelike portraits, was born in Antwerp. There, as a young student under Karel van Mander, he must have come into contact with the Rubens atelier. It is recorded that Rubens visited him in Holland in 1624.

Hals painted most of his noncommissioned works *alla prima* and with great freshness, catching the subject's likeness and fleeting expression with bold strokes. In these paintings he also used bold color, unlike his usual somber color schemes. In his commissioned works he showed more restraint, painting more carefully and in more than one sitting, although his brushwork is still bold, giving the effect of an *alla prima* painting. Many of Hals's portraits are unsigned; there is a story that quotes him as claiming his portraits needed no signature—his brushstroke was signature enough.

Hals, along wth Velasquez, was probably one of the greatest impressionists—in the true sense of the word. He realized that the viewer's eye travels toward the highlight, so Hals would leave great areas of shadow flat, allowing the viewer's mind to fill in the form. He was a master of simplification and suggestion.

Hals's palette was very simple, with only a few colors. He painted mostly with shades of gray. Unlike Rubens who painted from drawings, which gave him a chance to paint from a preconceived formula, Hals painted directly from life. He saw the shadows of the flesh as grayish, usually painting them in opaque color, and he achieved sparkle in his flesh tones by placing strong, warm highlights over a cool, gray middletone that covered his canvas. He saved his contrast in transparent and translucent areas for the clothes and background.

MEDIUM

Compared with the painting surfaces of Rubens and Rembrandt, Hals's surface does not seem to have thick *impastos* or thick globs of transparent medium in the dark accents. Although Hals could paint very directly, his commissioned works show a great deal of drybrush blending under the ultimate strong bravado strokes. There is no sign that the medium became tacky before the sitting was complete, so it seems that the drying time must have been a full day.

For this reason I use the same combination of the basic demonstration medium and beeswax medium that I use in the demonstrations for the techniques of Titian and Veronese. The recipes for these mediums can be found on pages 13 and 17.

PAINTING SURFACE

Hals painted predominantly on canvas tinted with a gray middletone, which was neither dark nor light. He was thus able to work directly toward darkness or light; white would show just as strongly against the gray as would burnt umber or black.

I paint this demonstration on a canvas mounted on a wood panel, as I do in preceding demonstrations. To prepare your canvas, follow the steps described in the section "Preparing Raw Canvas with White Lead" on page 24. When you have completed the final step and the surface is dry, paint on a final middletone of burnt umber, ivory black, white lead, and a little medium. When this is dry, the surface is ready for painting.

PROBABLE WORKING SEQUENCE

Hals's portraits were painted from life. He would first block in his portrait roughly in a warm tone, changing it until he had the correct proportions and placement. Then he would paint in the light middletone and the gray shadow. (When you paint from life, the shadow on flesh usually appears cool.) In Hals's work these two tones, opaque but not heavy, were worked back and forth with brushes until they were correct. The light was kept in a low key.

Once this step was finished, Hals would paint his higher lights and darker shadow accents. The shadow accents were often dark gray or black. Then he would blend the portrait with a dry brush, carefully modeling the form.

With bold strokes that looked like great slashes of paint—but were, in reality, carefully thought out strokes—Hals would apply the highlights and shadow accents, leaving them unblended to give the canvas a fresh and unlabored look.

If a second sitting was needed, Hals would start off with a *velatura* (translucent) middletone for the flesh, applied over the already dry flesh tone. He mixed this grayish flesh tone with medium, allowing the underpainting to show through. He would then proceed as if he were still in the first sitting, and he would paint into the *velatura* with opaque color.

This demonstration is painted *alla prima*.

COLORS AND BRUSHES

These are the colors I use, painting *alla prima*: white lead (flake white), yellow ochre light, French vermilion light, alizarin crimson, burnt umber, ivory black.

My brushes are numbers 5 and 8 round bristles, number 4 round sables, and small and large flat bristle blenders.

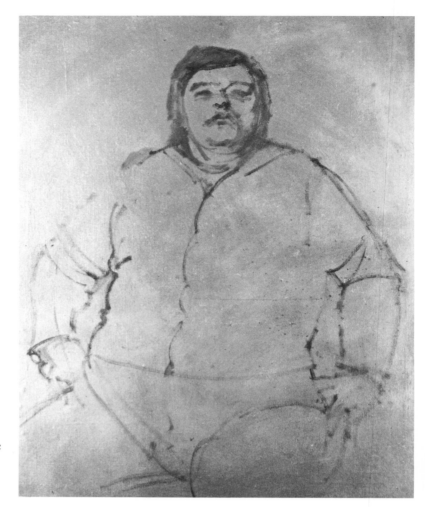

1.
Using burnt umber and a little medium on a brush, I sketch an outline of the subject. I sketch from life and paint directly on the canvas. The sketch is rough and I paint no details until the placement on the canvas is right.

2.
With the same thin mixture of burnt umber and medium, I paint in the shadow areas of the face and neck. With a brush I mix on the palette a middle flesh tone of yellow ochre, white, and a touch each of black and French vermilion, which I then apply with the same brush to the light areas of the face.

3.
I use a dark gray mixed from black and white to draw eyebrows and shadow accents. I then paint strong accents of French vermilion into the cheeks, nose, lips, and chin.

4.
I now mix a slightly lighter gray for the shadow areas of the face and neck, which seem cool when painting from life. I leave no empty spaces between the light and shadow areas; the shadow tone overlaps the light tone and creates a soft edge and not a sharp line. I reaffirm the shadow accents, and using a flat black tone, I paint in the hair.

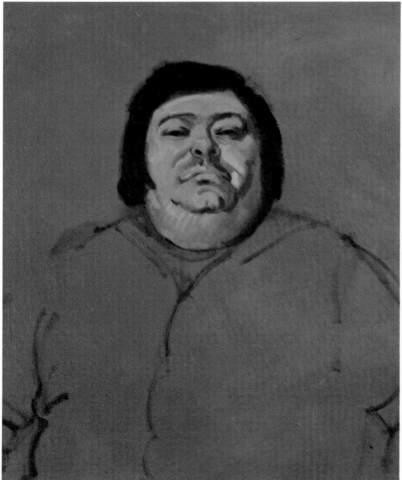

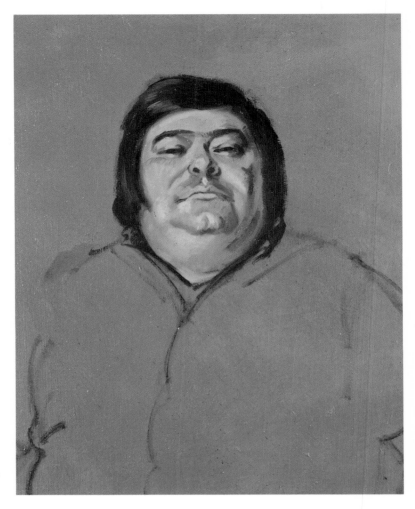

5.
I now add gray highlights to the
hair. As you can see, rendering
only the highlights on a dark surface is usually enough to establish
the texture. Using a mixture of
alizarin crimson and burnt umber, I paint the nostrils and the
line between the lips. I then blend
the face with a large, flat bristle
brush, carefully modeling forms
and softening edges. (If the drawing of the face is not correct at this
point, I can go back and make
corrections with the three basic
tones—middle flesh tones, gray
shadow tone, and dark shadow accent.)

6.
After making corrections, I now
boldly paint in highlights of
middle flesh tone and white, modeling these into the underlying
color. Then I carefully remodel
and soften the face, using the
brushes I have already been using
and the paint that is already
down. I do not apply any new
paint during this phase of modeling until I carefully place final
touches of highlights and dark accents and leave them unblended.
I do this to capture the freshness
of Hals' technique.

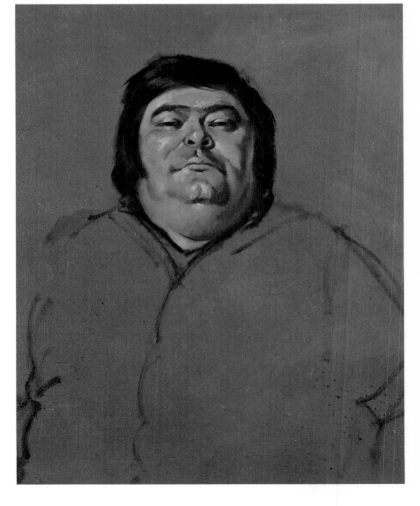

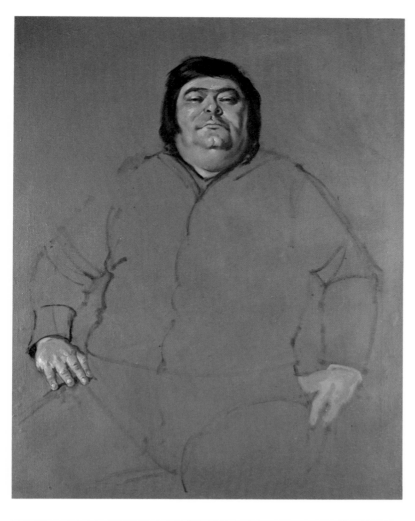

7.
I now paint in the sitter's right hand, following the same sequence I used for painting the head. I begin the left hand, using a mixture of yellow ochre, white, and a touch each of French vermilion and ivory black.

8.
I finish the hands, and with a mixture of yellow ochre, black, and a little medium, I begin painting in a thin background, leaving the canvas color showing through. Then, using only black, I paint the sweater.

9.
I scrub in the pants with a thin coat of burnt umber. Using a gray made of black and white, I paint the light areas of the sweater. Then I paint in the shadows with pure black. I finish covering the background and then blend it with a large, flat, dry bristle brush.

10.
I mix a lighter gray for highlights on both the sweater and the pants. I then paint into the underlying color with black and gray for shadows and I paint the collar with a light, flat, warm gray.

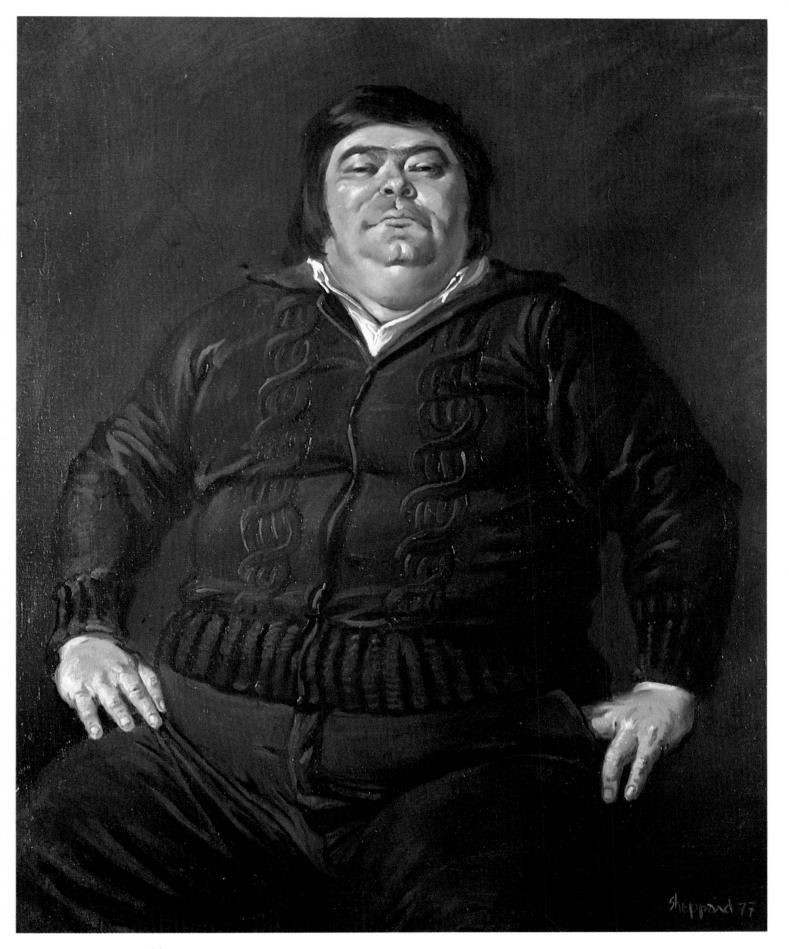

11.
I mark the highlights of the shirt with pure white and leave them unblended.
Using black for the shadows and gray for the highlights, I paint in the design on
the front of the sweater. I paint this demonstration *alla prima* in seven hours.

TECHNIQUES OF
REMBRANDT

Rembrandt van Rijn (1609–1669), known for his great, psychologically penetrating portraits, was born in Leyden and, as a young man, went to Amsterdam where he studied under Peter Lastman. Rembrandt's love of *chiaroscuro* must have begun here with his teacher, who had been to Italy and knew the works of Caravaggio.

Rembrandt's early paintings were executed thinly in the Dutch seventeenth-century style, but as he grew older, he exaggerated his technique, building the *impasto* heavier and heavier in the light and making his shadows more and more transparent.

Rembrandt's long series of self-portraits records the successes and failures of his career—as well as the development of his technique. He and Rubens were probably the two artists who knew most about the technique of oil painting. Both of them pushed to their limits the contrasts of transparencies and opacities, darks and lights, hard edges and *sfumato* edges, and warm colors and cool colors.

MEDIUM

Rembrant's medium, which seems to have been very thick, was probably a heavy jelly that became sticky or tacky very fast. Brushstrokes stand in high relief in the shadow areas of his paintings, which are transparent with dark tints of color. The light areas are equally thick but not transparent. His fast-drying medium produced his distinctive brushstrokes.

Whereas Rubens's strokes seem effortless, Rembrandt's seem to show a great struggle. Perhaps he did not have the drawing facility of Rubens; in any case, he corrected his drawing after the paint had already begun to grow tacky and resistant to the brush. The paint seems to have been put down and then corrected or moved with great difficulty, like taffy being pulled. This pushing and pulling of the sticky paint can be seen most clearly in the light areas of Rembrandt's paintings.

For this demonstration I use the variation of the basic medium, described on page 14. This is the same medium used in the demonstration of Rubens's technique.

PAINTING SURFACE

Rembrandt painted mainly on gray-toned canvas. There are some *alla prima* sketches on panels, but the major part of his work was painted in several sittings, for which canvas is better suited.

For this demonstration I mount canvas on ½″ plywood, which gives me the firmness of a panel and the texture of canvas. My canvas is prepared in the same way as the painting surface for the demonstration of Titian's technique. For instructions, refer to page 43. You can use this surface, or you can use stretched canvas. The final coat on the canvas should be an oil-paint mixture of raw umber, white lead, and medium. Paint this mixture on your canvas to create an undertone and to make the surface nonabsorbent. When this dries, your canvas is ready for painting.

PROBABLE WORKING SEQUENCE

Rembrandt painted most of his portraits from life. Because his figure drawing was not as facile as that of other great painters, he needed several sittings in which he could constantly correct to achieve his final product. He first sketched the portrait on the canvas with warm brown tones of oil paint and medium, rendering the transparent shadow areas with this color. He then painted an opaque, low-keyed skin tone into the light areas and modeled them with the shadows. He, like Rubens, emphasized powerful contrasts between transparent and opaque colors.

He used a cool gray—a mixture of black and white—for the turning points between shadow and light, often using on "optical gray," letting the gray of the canvas ground show instead of painting in gray tones. Because of yellowing varnish, these grays often appear green now.

He modeled the form together much like the *alla prima* painting of Rubens, working one tone back into another, correcting each form. Rembrandt constantly worked on contrasting his heavy opaque lights against his transparent medium-laden shadows, and his warm tones against his cool ones. He blended only after the paint had already become tacky and difficult to move, and this unusual texture became one of the qualities peculiar to the Rembrandt technique. However, he turned this quality—which would be a disaster for most painters—into his own special trademark. After a long sitting, when the paint would no longer move, he let the canvas dry.

Beginning a second sitting, Rembrandt would glaze the entire painting with medium and a tint of black or umber, immersing the entire subject in shadow. He would then take a cloth and carefully wipe out the light areas. Some of the glaze would remain in the crevices of the heavy *impasto* and make them seem even more three-dimensional. He would paint into this dark glaze. More often than not, he would not finish the painting until several similar sittings had taken place. The end result was a mysterious, soft, shadow effect with heavy layers of *impasto* emerging into the light.

COLORS AND BRUSHES

First sitting: white lead (flake white), yellow ochre light, French vermilion light, alizarin crimson, burnt sienna, burnt umber, ivory black. Second sitting: ivory black.

My brushes are numbers 4, 5, 6, 7, and 8 round bristles, number 5 round sables, and large and small flat bristle blenders.

1.
I roughly sketch in the subject on canvas with burnt umber and a little medium. Placement of the figure is the main concern at the beginning. I paint the portrait from life.

2.
Using burnt umber, I draw in the portrait more completely. I draw in the shadows transparently, handling the drawing as I would a watercolor wash drawing. I scrub in the background with yellow ochre, burnt sienna, and ivory black. I don't want the background color uniform, so I mix the paint directly on the canvas, using some colors more heavily than others.

3.
I now blend in the background with a large, dry, flat bristle brush, but I still don't make it uniform. Then I mix on the palette a flesh tone of yellow ochre, French vermilion, and a little white. Working with a bristle brush, I paint this tone into the light areas of the face and hands.

4.
With a gray—a mixture of ivory black and white that is almost the same value as the canvas—I paint in the shadow areas of the face. I also cover the beard with this gray.

5.
I now add touches of vermilion to the cheeks, nose, and knuckles to create deeper and stronger flesh tones.

6.
I redraw and correct shadows in the face with burnt umber.

7.
I paint in heavy, pure white on the beard and lay in an *impasto* mixture of yellow ochre and white on the head for the highlights.

8.
Using the bristle brushes I have already been painting with, I model areas where light and shadow meet. I first correct one color and then another with alternating brushes until the shapes are not only clearer, but also have softer edges.

9.
I lay a heavy white *impasto* on the beard and paint in lighter highlights on the head. I use a brush handle to scratch texture into the wet *impasto* of the beard. I also paint in details of the eyes and eyebrows and develop the hands further with a mixture of burnt umber and gray. I keep the highlights on the hands in a lower key than those of the head. Then, using burnt umber, I paint in the shadows of the coat, correcting and darkening them.

10.
I scrub in the shirt area with a dark tone. I darken this tone further by adding ivory black and then paint the pants with this mixture. I use ivory black for the shadows in the pants and a gray mixed with burnt umber for the highlights of the pants. I blend all these together with a large blending brush.

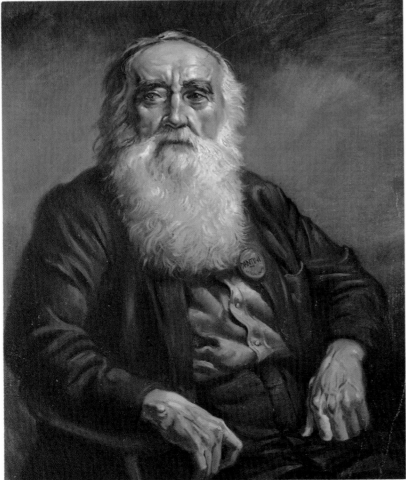

11.
I now use ivory black for the shadows of the shirt and a light gray for its highlights. I also paint in the shadows of the coat with ivory black.

12.
Using a mixture of burnt sienna and burnt umber, I paint this tone into the light area of the coat and blend the mixture into the shadow areas. I then use a heavy burnt sienna without any medium to mark in strongly the highlights on the coat. I leave the painting to dry for a few days. The time for the first sitting is approximately six hours.

13.
I begin the second sitting two days later. The paint has to be dry before I can apply a glaze to the background, or the first layer of paint will start to lift up. Using ivory black thinned with lots of medium, I now glaze over the background, letting it overlap the edges of the figure. You can see the wet, shiny glaze most clearly in the bottom half of the picture where the wet color reflects the glare of the light in my studio.

14.
Detail of finished painting. Although I did not follow the procedure here, many times after reaching the stage where the highlights had been wiped out in the face and beard, Rembrandt would work back into the head with opaque colors and repeat the various steps. This is essentially evident in his later work, which he painted with many more sittings.

15.
I blend in the background with a large, dry brush, letting the underpaint show through, and then paint over the rest of the figure and head with a coat of medium and just a touch of ivory black. I then blend this with a dry brush. I use a cloth to wipe out highlights on the face and beard. With this wiping out, the thin black glaze is forced down into the crevices of the brush strokes and gives the *impasto* an appearance of even more relief than it already has.

TECHNIQUES OF
VERMEER

Johannes Vermeer (1632–1675), born at Delft and now one of the most famous of the Dutch "little masters," was practically unknown until the last century. Only thirty to forty paintings have been attributed to him, a very small production for any artist.

His unique style, almost photographic, was magical in its representation of light and atmosphere. It could be said that he was the first photo realist, and it has been suggested that he painted with the aid of mirrors and other optical devices. Vermeer's images do have a photographic feeling; the distortion, perspective, and isolated highlights are those that one sees through a lens.

It is possible that he traced his image onto the canvas from a projection made with a *camera obscura*. Then he painted from life, either by looking at the subject through a lens or at a reflection in a mirror. There are no existing drawings by Vermeer. His painting *An Artist in a Studio* shows a very exact outline drawing on the gray canvas in the picture—the kind of drawing that one would make from a tracing, possibly with the aid of optical equipment.

Part of the charm and mystery of Vermeer's paintings lies in the atmosphere that he creates around his figures. He achieves this by using thin *velaturas* of color over a *grisaille* (gray) underpainting. Another special effect is his use of melting highlights: small dots of light seem to sparkle and sit above the form, yet their edges melt into the middletone without any signs of blending.

Vermeer was possibly the greatest painter of depth and atmospheric effects.

MEDIUM

Vermeer needed a medium that would enable him to blend well and keep his edges soft. Most of his paintings are small, so the need to cover large areas easily was not a consideration. Basically, he used a glaze technique, glazing colors over a very finished black-and-white underpainting. However, there had to be an ingredient in his medium that would automatically soften his brushstroke, letting it melt slightly without drybrush blending. Most likely, his medium was similar to that of Rubens but with the addition of Venice turpentine, which, when used sparingly, creates the melting effect that Vermeer was after.

For this demonstration I use the variation of my basic medium found on page 14. After packing the medium in the center of the palette, I put a few drops of Venice turpentine on the tip of a palette knife and mix this fluid into the medium. I also use a little of this medium—with its tiny amount of Venice turpentine—as a diluent, adding it to the paint with each brush stroke. When you try the Vermeer technique, please remember that *too much* Venice turpentine will cause the paint to run.

PAINTING SURFACE

Vermeer painted sometimes on canvas with a fine weave and a very smooth ground and sometimes on wood panels. He needed a very smooth finish for his highly precise technique. The color of the ground was gray, enabling him to add both dark and light tones immediately.

In this demonstration I use a panel of ¼″ untempered Masonite. To prepare the painting surface, I coat the smooth surface of the panel twice with acrylic gesso, sanding after each coat and moving my brush in a different direction for each coat. The coats are at right angles to one another. Then I paint on a final tone of 1 part acrylic matte medium and 1 part acrylic gesso. I tint this mixture with burnt umber and black pigment to achieve a medium gray. I allow the surface to dry before I start to paint.

PROBABLE WORKING SEQUENCE

I presume that Vermeer projected his image onto his gray canvas with a *camera obscura* and traced the outline with white chalk. (For my demonstration I work from several photographs, which I copy freehand.)

Once he had traced his outline, Vermeer rendered each form with grays made of black and white. He finished one section at a time, each time blending to make the form round and the edges soft. The total painting was executed in this fashion until everything looked finished but without color.

After the painting had dried, he went back for a second sitting, again using only black and white. In this sitting he painted *velaturas* of whites and grays to bring the light tones of the flesh and light-colored objects up to a higher key, preparing them for a glaze. A glaze is less effective—and less visible—if the underpainting is too dark.

In a third sitting he painted glazes and *velaturas* made of color and medium and then blended them with a dry brush.

Finally, Vermeer added the strongest highlights, light and opaque, consisting of medium, color, and a drop of Venice turpentine. The Venice turpentine softened the edge of the highlight stroke and produced a melted look that did not need any drybrush blending.

By using this technique, Vermeer could create an illusion of great depth and atmosphere.

COLORS AND BRUSHES

First and second sittings: white lead (flake white) ivory black. Third sitting: white lead, Naples yellow, yellow ochre light, French vermilion light, alizarin crimson, burnt umber, burnt sienna, ivory black, ultramarine blue.

My brushes are numbers 4, 5, 6, and 10 round bristles, number 6 round sables, medium and large flat bristle blenders, and ½″ flat oxhair blenders.

1.
Vermeer probably started by projecting an image directly onto his panel or canvas with the use of a *camera obscura*. For this demonstration I first make a drawing from several photographs and then trace it onto a panel with white chalk.

2.
Using grays made from ivory black, white, and medium, I paint in the flat tones: dark gray for the hair and ribbons and a middle-tone gray for the hat and shadow on the face. I leave the original tone of the canvas for the light areas.

3.
I now use a light gray for the light side of the face. The background tone overlaps the hair and the hat, creating soft edges.

4.
I cover the background with a light, flat gray, making some areas lighter than others. I then blend in all the forms with a large flat blending brush.

5.
Using a small sable brush, but still working only with grays, I draw the details of the face.

6.
I now paint bold white highlights into light-struck areas such as the top of the cheekbone, the chin, and the upper arm, following the contour of these forms.

7.
I blend in the highlights with a soft oxhair blender. Using a sable brush I restate the stronger highlights on the cheeks and nose with white. I then refine the details of the nose, eyes, and mouth with a darker gray.

8.
Painting with middletones of gray, I draw in the details of the hat and ribbon. I use pure white for the highlights and ivory black for the dark accents.

9.
I cover the rest of the canvas with my gray middletones and draw in the sitter's arms with dark gray accents. I change the position of the sitter's right arm from that in the original drawing, making it longer and moving it forward. I also add white to the light areas of the arms and hands, my strokes following the contours of the forms.

10.
I paint in the white highlights and dark gray accents of the drapery covering the sitter.

11.
Working with two sable brushes, I begin to define more precisely the different forms in the drapery and the headboard behind the sitter. I use one sable for the highlights and the other for the shadows. The undercoat of gray is still my middletone. I finish this first sitting in six hours, still using only ivory black and white.

12.
I now begin the second sitting. Using *velaturas* of white and gray, I paint halfpastes over the first sitting so that the underpainting shows through. I then blend these and restate the highlights and shadows as in the first sitting. It is necessary to bring up the tones of the lights to a higher key so that the glazes I put on later will be effective. Using only ivory black and white, I then blend and refine the painting until the *grisaille* underpainting is finished. This procedure is similar to the one I used in the demonstration of Titian's techniques. This ends the second sitting.

13.
I begin the third sitting with work on the background. I scrub a thin coat of medium over the gray underpainting and then paint in the scene behind the sitter in full color. I keep it subdued and in a low key. I glaze the drapery with Naples yellow and medium and add a touch of yellow ochre to the lower part to suggest shadow.

14.
I blend the drapery with a large, dry brush and glaze the hat with Naples yellow and medium. I glaze the shadow area under the brim with a mixture of yellow ochre, burnt umber, and medium and then blend the two tones. I use ultramarine blue and medium to glaze the ribbon.

15.
Using an opaque mixture of white, Naples yellow, and medium, I paint back into the highlights of the drapery and the hat. I then paint white, ultramarine blue, and medium on top of the blue ribbon to re-establish the design and the highlight. The few drops of Venice turpentine that I add to the medium diffuses the edges of these highlights so they will not need to be blended.

16.
I now glaze a mixture of burnt sienna, alizarin crimson, and medium over the headboard and blend it. Some of the color spills over the top left-hand corner, mixing with the background scene.

17.
I glaze a mixture of burnt umber and medium over the shadow area in the face, neck, chest and hair. Using a mixture of yellow ochre, vermilion, and medium, I glaze over the light areas of the flesh. I blend this second glaze with a dry brush. I also add vermilion tones to the cheeks.

18.
I blend in the flesh tones and paint highlight tones of yellow ochre and white into the glazed flesh. I then glaze the lips with a mixture of vermilion and alizarin crimson and place drops of white on the lips for highlights. I paint in the design on the pillow and glaze in the corners of the painting with a mixture of medium and a little ivory black. I then blend this glaze into the rest of the picture. This ends the third sitting.

19.
I finish the painting in this fourth sitting. I use my finger to rub final tints of alizarin crimson, vermilion, and medium into the cheeks and the shoulders. I then glaze the background, the pillow, and the corners of the painting with medium mixed with a touch of ivory black. Then I blend this area and wipe out the light area behind the head with a cloth.

GLOSSARY

Alla Prima. Direct painting without underpainting, with the painting completed in one sitting.

Beeswax. A natural wax, commercially available in either white or yellow form, often used as an additive in grinding pigments in oil; gives colors body and produces a matte look.

Black oil. Linseed or walnut oil that has been cooked with lead or litharge until black in color; used as the basis for various mediums.

Chiaroscuro. The contrast of light and shade and the art of distributing these elements in a picture.

Camera obscura. An apparatus usually operated with a mirror and double convex lens used to reflect an image which can be drawn or traced.

Cold pressed linseed oil. Oil extracted from flaxseed without the use of heat.

Drybrush painting. The technique of using a brush containing very little or no paint to blend or stipple paint that has been applied previously.

Gesso. A mixture of glue, water, and whiting used for priming a painting surface.

Glaze. A transparent coat of paint that enables a dry undercoat to show from underneath as through colored glass.

Grinding colors. A process of mixing dry pigment with medium or oil; can be done with a palette knife or muller on glass or a marble slab.

Grisaille. A painting rendered completely in black and white.

Halfpaste. See *velatura.*

Impasto. Heavily applied opaque paint that usually shows the marks of a brush, palette knife, or other tool for applying paint.

Litharge. A powdered form of lead, orange in color, used in making black oil.

Maroger, Jacques (1884-1962). Former Director of Restoration at the Louvre Museum in Paris; recipient of French Legion of Honor, 1937; former Professor of Art, Maryland Institute of Art, Baltimore; Author of *The Secret Formulas and Techniques of the Masters.*

Mastic varnish. A resin exuded from mastic trees that dissolves readily in turpentine or alcohol into a clear varnish; can also be incorporated into a painting medium; forms a jelly called *megilp* when mixed with linseed oil.

Mucilage. A grayish, gelatinous substance found in linseed oil; can be removed by a process known as "washing" in which water is mixed with oil and draws out the mucilage.

Powdered pigments. Pure color ground to a fine powder ready for mixing with a painting vehicle such as oil or water.

Sfumato. From the Italian word for smoked; a term used for soft, smokelike edges.

Tempera technique. Painting technique based on the use of opaque pigments ground with water and mixed with the yolk of egg.

Van Eyck medium. Oil medium, credited to Van Eyck, that was fluid enough to allow him to achieve subtle effects of light as well as precise rendering of detailed objects.

Velaturas. Translucent coat of paint that allows the dry undercoat to appear as through fog; sometimes called a halfpaste.

Washing oil. A process by which water is mixed with oil to draw out the mucilage.

Whiting. Calcium carbonate in a grayish or off-white powder form used as an inert pigment in gesso and some ceramic glazes; known as precipitated chalk if calcium carbonate is artificially prepared.

BIBLIOGRAPHY

Cennini, Cennino d'Andrea. *Il Libro dell 'Arte.* Translated by Daniel V. Thompson, Jr. as *Craftsman's Handbook.* New Haven: Yale University Press, 1933; New York: Dover Publications, 1954.

Cooke, Hereward Lester. *Painting Lessons from the Great Masters.* New York: Watson-Guptill Publications; London; Pitman Publishing.

Doerner, Max. *The Materials of the Artist and their Use in Painting.* Rev. ed. Translated by Eugen Neuhaus. New York: Harcourt, Brace, 1946.

Eastlake, Sir Charles Lock. *Methods and Materials of Painting of the Great Schools and Masters.* 2 vols. New York: Dover Publications, 1960.

Gettens, Rutherford J., and Stout, George L. *Painting Materials, A Short Encyclopaedia.* New York: Dover Publications, 1966.

Harley, R.D. *Artists' Pigments c. 1600-1835.* New York: American Elsevier Publishing, 1970.

Kay, Reed. *The Painter's Guide to Studio Methods and Materials.* New York: Doubleday, 1972.

Maroger, Jacques. *The Secret Formulas and Techniques of the Masters.* New York, London: Studio Publications, Inc., 1948.

Massey, Robert. *Formulas for Artists.* London: B.T. Batsford Ltd., 1968.

Mayer, Ralph. *A Dictionary of Art Terms and Techniques.* New York: Thomas Y. Crowell, Co., 1969.

Mayer, Ralph. *The Artist's Handbook of Materials and Techniques.* 3rd. ed. New York: Viking Press, 1970.

Taubes, Frederic. *The Painter's Dictionary of Materials and Methods.* New York: Watson-Guptill Publications, 1971.

Van Mander, Carel. *Dutch and Flemish Painters.* New York: McFarlane Ward, 1936.

Vasari, Giorgio. *On Technique.* G. Baldwin Brown, ed. Translated by Louisa S. Maclehose. London: J.M. Dent & Co., 1907; New York: Dover Publications, 1960.

INDEX

Edited by Connie Buckley
Designed by Jay Anning
Set in 11 point Baskerville